# BLACK
# STEM
# USA

## America's Next Civil Rights Movement

by

# C.M. WILLIAMS

with

## Sharon Ewell Foster

Published by C. M. Williams & Associates Press

For information about bulk purchases, contact C.M. Williams & Associates Press at 919-578-6343 or sales@blackstemusa.com. For information on booking an event, send requests to publicity@blackstemusa.com.

Cover and Interior Design: iMarketingPR

First American Paperback Edition, October 2015

Library of Congress Cataloging-in-Publication Data is available.

2015916467

Paperback: ISBN 0996870709

ISBN 978-0-9968707-0-2

# Contents

# Acknowledgements

First, I thank God for His guidance in the writing of this book. Without his guidance and leading, this book would not have been written.

I would like to thank Sharon Ewell Foster and Lanea Foster for their contributions to this book. Their mentorship through the final phases of this book's development was invaluable. I'd also like to thank them for having unshakeable faith that this book would be well received and help millions of people throughout the country. I thank them for introducing me to iMarketingPR who's expertise in designing the book helped make it a success.

To my sister, Wanda Williams and father, Junius Williams – thank you so much for your love and unconditional support as I undertook writing this book during one of the most challenging phases of my life.

My thanks also goes to Ms. Bea Stephens, Ms. Jackie Frazier, and my cousin Sharon Arrington for their insightful suggestion that my early research and writing about African Americans in technology be turned into a book. Without their prodding, I would never have attempted such an effort. I greatly appreciate their emails and phone messages sent to help encourage and keep me motivated through the project's completion.

Thanks also to Cynthia and James White who provided me with life coaching and encouraged me, along with others, to free my voice, stop hiding my God-given talent and gifts, and stand up bravely to be heard.

I would also like to thank Rhonda Hairston, Chase Taylor, Gregory Archer, Cecilia Barker, Greg Stoch, Susan Darby, Calvin Speight, Jr., Yvonne Cooper, Brenda Santos, Tangela Nesbitt Smalls, Bill Warner, James Stewart, Rev. Kenneth McDonald, Linda Lutz, Wake Technology Community College Continuing Education instructors, Carlene Hill Byron, and the numerous other friends and supporters who helped me by providing emails and 1-on-1 sessions filled with ideas for content development, branding, and marketing of this book. Your encouraging comments, objective critiques, and suggestions about the information communicated in this book were insightful and appreciated.

Finally, I'd like to thank all the teachers, instructors, college faculty and administrative staff, mentors and sponsors that helped me along the way to becoming a lover of all things STEM and a successful contributor to the world of STEM. Although I wanted to be a lawyer when I was young, I do not regret going into engineering. Even with all of the difficulties that I faced throughout my career, I can proudly say that I got to be a major contributor to some of the greatest technical inventions and initiatives of the 21$^{st}$ century. These experiences were the result of the individuals throughout my life who paved the way and lifted me upon their shoulders to achieve more than I thought was possible.

A special thanks to the Durham North Carolina Public Library System and my local Starbucks® where I spent countless hours using their free Wi-Fi, typing, and doing research. These two entities were a godsend to me in this effort.

--C.W. Williams

September 2015

I write this while a ninth-grader, Ahmed Mohamed, an engineering genius has been arrested in Irving, Texas, for bringing an alarm clock he designed to school to show to his teachers. Son of a Sudanese engineer who works for NASA, young Ahmed was taken into custody after teachers, his principal, and Irving police were frightened that the youth had created a bomb that would harm them. Arrested in front of his schoolmates and teachers, Ahmed was taken into custody, handcuffed, and interrogated by police. Sensitive to the fact that the overreaction of Irving authorities because of Ahmed's color and Muslim heritage might discourage other brilliant young minds, the hashtags #IstandwithAhmed and #helpAhmedmake were trending across the country and

7

caught the eyes of President Barak Obama, Secretary of State Hilary Clinton, as well as Facebook founder and CEO Mark Zuckerberg who reached out to encourage the lad. All the while, #BlackLivesMatter continues to draw attention to the struggles of young blacks in America.

C.M. Williams presented at a writers workshop looking for coaching with a manuscript under development. I subsequently learned that Williams was an engineer and that the book was about STEM (science, technology, engineering, and math) and about black folks' presence, or lack thereof, in the STEM world. What I read hit a nerve and brought clarity to my own STEM experiences. I was one of the students Williams writes about: I transferred from STEM studies to major in the humanities.

Though I left high school intending to major in graphic art, because I was a National Merit scholar and had pretty good math and science grades, I was encouraged to major in engineering. When I stepped into my first engineering seminar, I don't recollect seeing another black face, certainly not another black female face. I do recall, however, that hundreds of young white males turned, gaping at me. I was an oddity, but it never occurred to me that my efforts to become an engineer would spark hostility among those who were charged with educating me. I wasn't wanted. By semester's end, I had switched my major.

Once I made the decision, I rarely looked back. However, life serendipitously seemed to move me in and around the STEM world, where I worked with engineers and scientists as a systems analyst, a logistician, and as a technical writer. Williams' brilliant conceptualization of STEM as a civil rights movement helped me understand my own experiences. As part of my contribution, I reached out to others I knew who either worked in STEM fields or who were STEM-trained. It was shocking how much their experiences mirrored my own—even those who attended school twenty or more years after I did.

The credit for this book's concept goes to C.M. Williams. This book is the culmination of years of Williams' effort and research; the chapters on startups and funding have only been lightly touched. There was so much material, one of the most difficult tasks was deciding what to keep and what to discard. I did what a good technical writer does: I fleshed out the engineer's concept and worked to make it accessible to the lay reader. The manuscript has been restructured, I have added text and rewritten some. Following Williams' vision, I worked to flesh out the history and to tie the thread of STEM to the Civil Rights movement. When I challenged Williams to share from the heart and reveal personal insights about STEM education and the culture, the author was fearless and generous. Because of my own experiences, I worked to offer plans that might help students, families, churches, communities, organizations, and corporations work together to improve Black STEM outcomes.

Thanks to God for this opportunity to serve and for all the twists and turns of my life which have made me who I am. Thank you to my son and daughter, Chase and Lanea, for reading the manuscript and encouraging me. Thank you to those, like Computer Systems Engineer/Software Developer and IT Program Manager Gloria Anderson Riddick and Statistician Pamela Taylor, who generously shared their STEM stories and helped make this a better book. Thank you, also to pastors Bishop Walter Scott Thomas, Sr., Reverend James T. Meeks, and Bishop Howard Oby. Thank you for inspiring me, for providing hope and vision for your congregations, and for being education champions for the people of the cities in which you reside.

My hope is that this book will make a difference and encourage bright minds (young and old) to find room at the table. A change is gonna come.

Sharon Ewell Foster

September, 2015

# Introduction

*"I do feel, in my dreamings
and yearnings, so
undiscovered by those
who are able to help me."*

~ Mary McLeod Bethune, Educator and
Founder of Bethune –Cookman College

I have always had a deep desire to do something to help the ethnic community of which I am a part by using the gifts and talents that I possess. My desire to give back was natural because of a feeling deep down inside that this was my life's purpose. I have a deep sense of social justice because of the many difficulties in my life and the greater difficulties of black people who do not have the resources or experiences I've had. I do not want to see black people…my people…suffer. What started out as a personal memo to myself, grew into a mini-proposal with a former friend. That mini-proposal turned into a white paper created out of curiosity and for fun. That white paper, finally, after much

12

research and deliberation, evolved into this book. Something inside of me would not let go of the passion I experienced in writing about the subject of black America's possible untapped prosperity gained through embracing new technology development and creative financial investing for the 21$^{st}$ century. This book is the result.

America is losing ground in the global STEM war (science, technology, engineering and math). According to National Math and Science Initiative Statistics:

- By 2009, for the first time, over half of U.S. patents were awarded to non-U.S. companies because STEM shortcomings are forcing a hold on innovation.

- The U.S. may be short as many as three million high-skilled workers by 2018.

America is losing ground in the global STEM wars, in part, because Black America's creative genius is missing in action. The same innovative thinking that birthed jazz, the same creative thinking that developed more than 300 uses for the peanut, is what's needed to help solve the technological issues facing the world. According to its current trajectory, despite its gifts and talents, black America is being left behind as a major player in the world's technological advancement.

A 21$^{st}$ century revolution in thought and action is needed in the black community. Dr. Joyce Brothers once said, "Trust your hunches. They're usually based on facts filed away just below the conscious level." Well, I have a hunch that there are many people out there who think like I do and believe that if blacks can better organize themselves in the areas of technology, business, and finance, many of our economic and social challenges could be overcome. Revolutionary action and thought are needed to make this change happen. The change must be based upon valid existing data, driving more comprehensively constructed strategies, to achieve more tangible and sustainable economic and financial outcomes. This new approach needs to maximize its use of the physical and virtual resources in existence today. This thought revolution requires a uniting of the generations (i.e. youth with computer and digital media skills working with more senior individuals in the black community who have years of business expertise and industry acumen, etc.) to change. It will also require different skill sets and experiences to make it happen.

During the course of writing this book, three major events related to African Americans and people of African descent occurred that significantly impacted the concepts presented in this book. The first event was the celebration by Americans of all colors, races, and ethnicities of the 50th anniversary of the Civil Rights Movement's March on Washington held on August 28, 1963. In addition to my possessing a personal interest in the sciences, economics, and finance, I have always been a history buff. So watching the march's remembrance on TV was compelling and applicable to the ideas captured here. The March on Washington, a seminal event for African Americans and the country, took a great deal of planning, organizing, motivating, and mobilizing. Just as in 1963, over 200,000 people attended the 50<sup>th</sup> anniversary activities that took place at the Lincoln Memorial in Washington, DC. The original March on Washington was architected by a group of individuals who understood the paramount need to address the plight of disenfranchised African Americans in new and creative ways. The execution of the massive original march was a reminder that once black Americans put their minds and efforts towards an initiative of profound importance, they have the fortitude to undertake it with incredible positive results. That same fortitude and relentless work is what's needed to improve the lives of every African American in today's new global economy. The anniversary recreation was a joyous reminder of that power and ability.

The second major event influencing my work on this book was the death of former South African president, Nelson Rolihlahla Mandela. Nelson Mandela was world renowned for the roles he played in leading his country, South Africa, away from the vestiges of racial apartheid to a new democratic society of equality between the races, with economic improvements for the country's black Africans. Past generations, like Nelson Mandela's, worked to advance the political, social, and economic positions of the people of African descent. His death, at the age of 95 years old, reminded many around the world of his efforts, like those of the leaders of the American Civil Rights, to gain equality through changing laws that hindered black people's lives. Mandela worked to make sure that his dark African citizens had a solid foundation for economic equality as well. His accomplishments enabled the reclamation of some of the native lands that had been taken from the African people during European colonization. After becoming president, his leadership actions were done in a nonviolent way through acts of reconciliation with white South Africans. His actions helped ensure black South Africans would have the best chance possible to succeed economically in their newly organized country. This strategy has resulted in South Africa continuing to be a major economic powerhouse on the African continent. Thoughts of Nelson Mandela's concepts of inclusive African economic equality helped to formulate some of the recommended approaches articulated later in this book.

The third and final event that greatly influenced the content of this book was the death of another great icon of African America, Dr. Maya Angelou.  At the age of 86 years old, Ms. Angelou left this world going home to the next. People of all nations and backgrounds mourned the loss of a wise, insightful, and spirit-filled woman. The poet and author presented an example of how black Americans can change the world around them based upon their writings. Ms. Angelou's literature provides relevant context for understanding the complex cocktail of economic, social, and political disparities affecting African Americans in a way that is understandable, relatable, and emotionally engaging. This manner of writing and communicating new ideas to an African American audience became my goal and helped to increase the need to include illustrations and graphs. Dr. Angelou's example helped me to better construct the variety of avenues for explaining and demonstrating more specifically the current economic and financial barriers, as well as "hidden" opportunities, that black Americans face in overcoming their 21$^{st}$ century struggles.

Many African Americans have begun to lament what may become the accelerated destruction of the black community. The deaths of leaders like South Africa's Mandela and the United States' Angelou, and celebrations of significant past accomplishments, like the March on Washington, have added a subtle urgency to this lamentation. Black academics, politicians, religious leaders, and average black citizens are searching for the next wave of activists to step forward to help move the black collective forward.

There must be recognition that the tools of yesterday (i.e. marches, protests, campaigns to get changes in laws and governing policies, etc.) may not be the most effective tools for the issues black Americans face today. New strategies and approaches to attaining increased equality in today's globally connected and technologically driven world are needed. Instead of simply asking where the next leaders lie, African

Americans must begin to organize themselves around finding answers to the following two questions:

- What actions are needed for blacks to succeed in today's 21$^{st}$ global technological society?

- How can blacks mobilize to quickly put these actions into place?

The solutions to these two questions must be instituted soon before America loses the STEM wars and before black America becomes a permanent underclass in this new world. So, I've written this book for moms and dads, teachers, pastors, churches, organizations—for folks who want to learn about STEM and how we can help turn the tide on things— how we can help ourselves. It is hoped that some of the solutions are described here in this "memo" to my community. It is also for corporate America, with notes on how it might help.

--C.M. Williams

# Chapter 1:
# Our Present Urgency

*"You must change in order*
*to survive."*

~ Pearl Mae Bailey
American Actress and Singer

As we waited for choir rehearsal to begin, one of my fellow choir members, a deacon, said, "Our community is in trouble and everybody knows it!" His statement echoed the consensus of the little group of black church goers who had gathered early for rehearsal.

The choir had been organized almost since the church's beginning and its members were some of the church's most senior congregants. Over 600 years of wisdom was corralled in the room. The little group had been discussing various recent news stories about the state of the local black citizenry in South Carolina. I found their insights fascinating. As a former GM technology executive, I shared their frustration.

What my fellow choir members didn't know, was that it had been my good fortune to lead an automotive engineering team. I was a corporate insider employed in the science, technology, engineering, and math (STEM) fields. GM has made great strides, but I was employed there, along with Mary Barra and a handful of other hardworking self-sacrificing women, when the thought of a female or black executive officer or senior vice president was rare and seemingly impossible. I had the good life: jet-setting around the world, expensive car, expensive home, nice clothes.

But the combination of a declining American automotive industry and my aging parents' physical decline, had taken me from Detroit and led me back to Durham, North Carolina, with little to show for my years as a workaholic. Armed with my advanced engineering degree and decades of experience, as things settled with my parents, I returned to the work world. There was a cry for blacks in STEM; I thought I'd be off and running in no time. But it was not easy. I'd be rich if I counted the number of times I heard, "You're overqualified." Or, "You're too inexperienced."

It took over a year, but I landed a job as a contractor working on a health care information technology project for the state of South Carolina. The pay cut my former salary in half, but I was grateful and enjoyed the work. I successfully completed the work, but, now, once again, I was jobless.

For seven years, I had been unable to obtain permanent employment anywhere and the humiliation, embarrassment, depression, loneliness, and frustration of the circumstance was beginning to take a major toll on my life. I was beginning to feel that all of the gifts I had acquired in my life were some kind of hideous torture by God. I was using my talents to help other people achieve their dreams, but none of mine were coming true. But the conversation the choir members were having around me was a tap on the shoulder to stop focusing on myself and instead concentrate on helping to find solutions for the more urgent needs of my ethnic brothers and sisters.

"Yes, sir," affirmed another elderly choir member as she rocked side to side in her folding chair while listening to the deacon. As she rocked, her trancelike gaze seemed to penetrate the walls of the rehearsal room. "Things aren't like they used to be and they're not getting any better," the deacon continued. "These black folks today are in the street doing all kinds of things and having all kinds of things done to them; things that we never thought of doing when we were their age." Several members of the group quietly nodded their heads in agreement. "And they're experiencing things people my age experienced back in the days of segregation. None of this nonsense is focused on what they should be concerned with – the future. THEIR future. OUR community's future. Something's gotta change. Yes, Lord!" he shouted. He stopped preaching as more people entered the room. I sat there anxious to hear the rest of the deacon's comments. However, just as another group member was about to interject her thoughts into the group's conversation, the choir director greeted the group as the rehearsal formally began

While we sang, my mind raced back over the previous discussion. The topic and the consensus of the group about the ailing modern-day African-American condition captured my problem-solving imagination. "If we all agree about our community's position," I thought, "then why are we not doing anything ourselves about it? Unemployment. Poverty. Police brutality. Frustration. Division. What *could* we do about it?" I had knowledge and experience as an insider, as an African American insider. I could help. I resolved to help find the solution.

As the rest of the world gallops forth headstrong into a new global and technological society, no one has to tell blacks that their community is in a state of crisis and being left behind. According to a 2013 report by the US Census Bureau, African Americans comprise 14% of the US population, but only 3% of the STEM workforce as compared to 13% of the total US workforce[i]. This workforce percentage is far behind corresponding percentages for white (63%), and Asian Americans, which includes people of Indian descent (27%). Hispanics have surpassed blacks and represent 7% of the US STEM workforce.

What is STEM? "STEM" is an acronym standing for *science, technology, engineering,* and *mathematics.* It is the group of studies and work involved with the sciences and technical innovations. The four areas are interconnected in their problem-solving and critical thinking requirements. It is for this reason that the four areas are combined when referenced. For most people it takes many years of formal study to acquire adequate skills in science, math, engineering, and technology, starting when they are children. Individuals with strong skills in these four areas often become inventors. Wealth, for a growing number of nations, is rarely being generated from physical or manual labor by its citizens. Today's society and economy is based upon the ability to create innovations. Being an inventor can be a direct pathway to wealth and prosperity. This is why the acronym STEM has become important. When policy makers and industry leaders talk about the skill sets needed to work in today's knowledge-based society, they most often refer to it as "a need for STEM".

For much of my career, I was an insider in the STEM world. So I know firsthand how few African American's are able to sit at the table and enjoy the fruits of our new knowledge-based society. This exclusion is a threat to the future economic health of the country.

Each new national report on the financial and economic decline of African-Americans is further proof that the black portion of America, as a whole, is not enjoying the growing prosperity derived from profitable participation in the technology expansions occurring in the US and around the world. Today's prosperity comes from skills in STEM. In the new world, driven by STEM, African Americans are missing in action. There appears to be a mismatch between African-American capabilities and their ability to produce in the rapidly evolving technical and knowledge-based society.

27

There are many explanations for the lack of black American STEM presence. Willie Pearson, Jr. was a professor of sociology at the School of History, Technology, and Society, Georgia Institute of Technology. Prior to joining the faculty at Georgia Tech as chair of the School of History, Technology and Society in July 2001, he held a distinguished appointment as Wake Forest Professor of Sociology at Wake Forest University and an adjunct position in medical education at Wake Forest University School of Medicine. In his 1985 study entitled "Black Scientists, White Society, Colorless Science: A Study of Universalism in American Science" (Associated Faculty Press), Willie Pearson, Jr., gave the following reasons for the low numbers of African- Americans in science: (1) lack of early encouragement and motivation (24.4 percent); (2) lack of financial support and limited opportunities (15.1 percent); (3) limited recruitment (11.2 percent) and institutional racism (11.2 percent); (4) lack of tradition (8.7 percent); and (5) science perceived as too difficult and unrewarding and lack of role models (8.3 percent each). In this book, we will address the following problems.

# BLACK STEM PROBLEMS

1. Lack of equity in education and inadequate early career guidance;

2. Non-black STEM worldview in

   - many families
   - K-12 schools
   - the media
   - African American communities;

3. Lack of black STEM role models to help teach, mentor, and advocate for Black STEM college students;

4. Few Black STEM students pursuing advanced graduate and post-graduate degrees in technology;

5. Excessive diversion of young blacks into the corporatized incarceration system;

6. Legitimate concerns about racism in the hiring and promotion practices of technology companies;

7. Funneling of Black-STEM employees out of the pipeline that leads to the boardroom;

8. Lack of black technology entrepreneurs, perpetuating the crippling cycle of limited black innovation leadership in STEM;

9. Lack of financial resources and structure; and

10. Finally, there are still pundits and armchair quarterbacks that believe black America's STEM problem lies with the ethnic group's inferiority, lack of gumption and initiative. They are willing to do nothing to support change. Their sideline activities are harmful and impede progress.

In the chapters that follow, we will explore these problems and offer solutions and recommendations for a holistic strategy that advances African Americans in STEM and survival in the new global economy.

Billions of dollars and millions of jobs, like software developers, bioengineers, and technical writers, are being generated by the new technology reality while a majority of black people stand on the sidelines. Unless something changes, the US black community (as a whole) will further decline; its ability to catch up and participate in the technology race lost in the smoldering embers of a technology race that has ended, without hope of ever regaining ground.

"Something's gotta change!" the deacon's voice echoes. With change, there is hope.

Without many people realizing it, a speeding up of the technology race is underway. With more concentrated focus, better use of available resources, and a comprehensive work effort (i.e. a new civil rights movement 2.0), the African-

American technology involvement picture can be completely altered.

There is a saying that the definition of insanity is doing the same thing repeatedly expecting a different response. We must do something different if the picture for blacks is to change. It is time for African Americans to take a different role and steps to get into the 21$^{st}$ century's innovation and technology race. While blacks have mastered *embracing* products of STEM activities as *consumers*, we must now master innovation and production. We must insist on being recognized for our achievements. We must insist on a place at the STEM table. Our activity as producers of technology needs a major effort, like the Civil Rights Movement of 50 years ago.

Our STEM presence is vital to our community.

Our STEM presence is vital to corporate America.

Black STEM presence is vital to our nation's security and prosperity.

Ready or not, it's time for a change. The steps to bring about that change begin with this book.

So, first, let's look at history to see how we got to where we are today.

# Chapter 2:
# The History of Black Technology

*". . . the people commonly called Negroes, Indians, mulattoes and mustizoes, have been deemed absolute slaves, and the subjects of property in the hands of the particular persons. . ."*

~ Slave Code of South Carolina, May 1740

Throughout America's history, African-Americans lacked the opportunity to take advantage of the technological advancements occurring in society. Let's explore the history of STEM in Africa and of Africans in America.

Many of us, despite not being taught of them in school, have heard about great African kingdoms like Timbuktu. We have heard of ancient markets and trade routes in Western and Eastern Africa. However, much less is known about STEM in ancient Africa. Scholarship biased by colonial views has long negated and overlooked the contributions of Africans to science and technology. But the work of renowned scholars like Ivan Van Sertima and Dr. Charles Finch, MD, offers insight and begins to close this gap.

The late Dr. Van Sertima was educated at the School of Oriental and African Studies (London University) and at Rutgers Graduate School and held degrees in African Studies and Anthropology. Professor of African Studies at Rutgers University, Dr. Van Sertima was also Visiting Professor at Princeton University. He was editor of the *Journal of African Civilizations* and published several major anthologies which included *Blacks in Science: Ancient and Modern*.

In an essay entitled *The Lost Sciences of Africa: An Overview*, Dr. Van Sertima, who lectured at more than 100 universities in the United States, Canada, the Caribbean, South America and Europe, wrote:

> *In 1978 anthropology professor, Peter Schmidt, and professor of engineering, Donald Avery, both of Brown University, announced to the world that, between 1,500-2,000 years ago, Africans living on the western*

34

*shores of Lake Victoria, in Tanzania, had produced carbon steel.*

*The Africans had done this in pre-heated forced-draft furnaces, a method that was technologically more sophisticated than any developed in Europe until the mid-19th century. "We have found," said Professor Schmidt, "a technological process in the African Iron Age which is exceedingly complex....To be able to say that a technologically superior culture developed in Africa more than 1,500 years ago overturns popular and scholarly ideas that technological sophistication developed in Europe and in Africa."*

*There were Africans still living (the Haya people, for example) who, although they no longer produced steel, remembered, down to the last identity of detail, the machine and the process their ancestors used and were able to reconstruct the furnace and carry out a successful smelt. When Schmidt and Avery began excavating near Lake Victoria and dug up 13 Iron Age furnaces, they found that "the construction of furnaces*

*and the composition of the steel was essentially the*

*same."*

Dr. Finch, formerly the Director of International Health at

the Morehouse School of Medicine, in Nashville, is a graduate

of Yale University and a 1976 graduate of Jefferson Medical

College.  He completed a family medicine residency at

the University of California Irvine Medical Center in 1979. In

the 1980s, he published more than a dozen articles, including

*The African Background of Medical Science and Science and*

*Symbol in Egyptian Medicine.* A collection of Dr. Finch's

essays, *The African Background to Medical Science,* was

published by Karnak House (London) in November, 1990. His

well-documented work details surgeries where African doctors

"attained a level of skill comparable with, and in some

respects superior to" Western 20th century surgeons. One of

the most impressive of these was a Caesarean operation

performed by East African Banyoro surgeons. The operation

was witnessed and sketched by Dr. Robert Felkin, a

missionary doctor, in 1879. According to Finch, at a time when operations were rare in Europe, the skills demonstrated in this operation startled readers of the Edinburgh Medical Journal where it was reported. The African surgeon used antiseptic surgery, showed an understanding of the sophisticated concepts of anesthesia and antisepsis, and demonstrated advanced surgical techniques, especially in his cautious use of the cautery iron, said Dr. Finch.

Prior to the colonial period, there were African advances in metallurgy, mathematics, astronomy, architecture and engineering. For example, a June 2013 article by Eric A. Powell, entitled *Miniature Pyramids of Sudan*, in *Archaeology Magazine*, tells the story of African pyramids built as early as 300 B.C. Then there are the castles and cathedrals of Ethiopia, also erected long before the Colonial period. Most fascinating are the churches of Lalibela. A June 2013 CNN article by Errol Barnett, entitled *Rock churches of Lalibela, the Jerusalem of Ethiopia*, shares details about the 11 rock-hewn churches, or cathedrals, constructed in northern Ethiopia over

900 years ago. The churches, connected by a complex system of tunnels, drainage ditches, and tunnels are still in use. Barnett quotes Alebachev Retta, an 86-year-old church scholar, who explains what makes the Lalibela churches such wonders. "They are different because they were built from the top down," [Retta] says. "Everywhere in the world, structures are built from the ground up. There is nothing comparable in the world." (View photos of the Lalibela churches at http://www.cnn.com/2013/06/27/travel/rock-churches-lalibela-ethiopia/index.html and http://www.photosbymartin.com/africa/ethiopia_lalibela_pictures.htm)

With such a rich history of technology behind us, it is hard to believe that Africans in America would not evidence some leanings toward innovation. The reality is, that though their accomplishments are rarely recorded in school books, there were many early African American innovators. Among them are:

**Benjamin Banneker** - farmer, inventor, mathematician, astronomer, almanac publisher and land surveyor. Slave owner Thomas Jefferson recommended Banneker, a free man of color, to be a part of a surveying team to lay out Washington, D.C. Appointed by President George Washington, Banneker saved the project when the lead architect quit–taking all the plans with him. Banneker was able to recreate the plans.

**Judy W. Reed** - patented a hand-operated machine for kneading and rolling dough. On September 23, 1884, she became the first known African-American woman, though she could not sign her name, to obtain a patent.

**Nat Turner** - leader of the 1831 slave uprising in Southampton County, was also credited as having an interest in STEM. In the flawed pamphlet, published in 1831, *The Confessions of Nat Turner*, author Thomas Gray quotes Nat Turner, ". . . all my time, not devoted to my master's service, was spent either in prayer, or in making experiments in casting different things in moulds [sic] made of earth, in attempting to make paper, gunpowder, and many other experiments," Turner is quoted as confessing in Gray's pamphlet.

**Annie Malone** - was inventor, founder and owner of Poro College, a cosmetics firm that started in St. Louis (@1902) and later occupied an entire city block in Chicago. Madam C.J. Walker worked as a Poro agent in 1905.

**Madam C. J. Walker** - was inventor, pioneer of the modern black hair-care and cosmetics industry, and self-made millionaire.

**Thomas Jennings** - born in 1791, is believed to have been the first Black inventor to receive a patent. The patent, awarded on March 3, 1821, was for his discovery of a process called dry-scouring which was the forerunner of today's modern dry-cleaning. A free tradesman, he operated a dry cleaning business in New York City. An abolitionist, in 1831 he became assistant secretary for the First Annual Convention of the People of Color in Philadelphia, PA.

**Henry Blair** - was the second black inventor issued a patent. Blair, born in Maryland around 1807, received patents on October 14, 1834 for a seed planter and in 1836 for a cotton planter.

Though slaves were prohibited from receiving patents on their inventions, by 1913 over a thousand patents had been issued to African Americans.

Many African Americans, including our children, are crippled by a historical perspective that depicts Africans as wild savages, people who were barely human, brought to America to be civilized. We must challenge the veracity of what we've been taught. Slavers didn't check the credentials of the enslaved. They didn't inquire about religious associations, education, family status, or work history. Slavers didn't check to see if those they captured were fluent in multiple languages or if they were teachers, architects, or healers. They did not ask if those who were enslaved were literate. Slavers did not want to know; they simply wanted to sell human beings for money. They stripped the enslaved of

41

their clothes, languages, and identities. The truth is some enslaved people were farmers who brought with them skills and agricultural acumen learned in Africa. Some were likely Christian and Muslim. Some were likely smiths, teachers and doctors or healers. The truth is, that Europeans would not have paid for slaves and fought to keep them in captivity if they were bungling idiots. Though they were not paid for their labor, enslaved people built roads, managed farms, and built much of our nation's early capital. They were intelligent enough that childrearing was given, many times, into their exclusive care; this is not work given to fools, lest the child become a fool. At least one free African American, Benjamin Banneker as mentioned earlier, like the story of Joseph in Egypt, helped lead in Washington DC's architectural design when it was most critical. Others like Solomon Northup, whose biography, *Twelve Years a Slave*, was recently turned into an award-winning movie, provided innovations that benefitted slave owners, though he, the enslaved person, was never given credit or payment. Instead of being ashamed of them or discounting their contributions, our nation owes of debt of gratitude to the millions of enslaved people who helped build and establish this nation, despite all they suffered. They are heroes.

Almost twenty years after Finch and Van Sertima's research, Clapperton Chakanetsa Mavhunga, an associate professor in MIT's Program in Science, Technology, and Society, continues to challenge scholarship that describes Africans as passive consumers of technology and not as innovators. His book, "Transient Workspaces: Technologies of Everyday Innovation in Zimbabwe" (MIT Press, September 2014), shares insight about technology in the border region where Zimbabwe, Mozambique, and South Africa meet. A book description states:

*In this book, Clapperton Mavhunga views technology in Africa from an African perspective, a perspective that includes spirituality. Technology in his account is not something always brought in from outside, but is also something that ordinary people understand, make, and practice through their everyday innovations . . .*

*Technology does not always originate in the laboratory in a Western-style building but also in the society, in the forest, in the crop field, and in other places where knowledge is made and turned into practical outcomes. African creativities are found in African mobilities. Mavhunga shows the movement of people as not merely conveyances across space but transient workspaces.*

Though many Westerners consider science and faith mutually exclusive, African notions of technology are closely married with spirituality. African advances are born of the people and not confined to labs. In an *MIT News* October 2014 interview and review of Mavhunga's book, entitled *The Overlooked History of African Technology*, the author, Peter Dizikes quotes Mavhunga, "What I am challenging is the idea that technology can only come from outside Africa, from the laboratories and factories," Mavhunga says. "This general narrative of technology transfer — from the haves to the have-nots — is one I find troubling." Mavhunga further asserts,

"Western scholars talk about technology in the Roman Empire," Mavhunga says. "If we say that technology is something that comes prior to the colonial period, what does it do to the way we think about history?"

Indeed. To continue to record and teach a history that excludes an entire continent as a source of innovation and technology is lazy scholarship hobbled by the chains of colonialism. It is a hindrance to future Black STEM scholars who grow up saddled with a world view that excludes people who look like them from discussions of ancient technology and innovation. It is a hindrance to corporate executives and leaders who are trained in a world that blinds them to seeing the color black.

**Rooted in the past**

With a rich history of entrepreneurship and STEM, what has stifled African American entrepreneurship and developments in STEM? Perhaps the answer can be found in documents like the South Carolina Slave Code, which predates even the birth of our nation.

*XXX. And be it further enacted by the authority*

*aforesaid, That no slave who shall dwell, reside, inhabit*

*or be usually employed in Charlestown, shall presume*

*to buy, sell, deal, traffic, barter, exchange or use*

*commerce for any goods, wares, provisions, grain,*

*victuals, or commodities, of any sort or kind*

*whatsoever. . . (Excerpt from South Carolina Slave*

*Code of 1740)*

*XXI. And be it further enacted by the authority*

*aforesaid, That no slave or slaves whatsoever,*

*belonging to Charlestown, shall be permitted to buy*

*any thing to sell again, or to sell any thing upon their*

*own account. . . (Excerpt from South Carolina Slave*

*Code of 1740)*

Laws like the May 1740 Slave Code of South Carolina

criminalized black entrepreneurship and codified the notion

that blacks should "stay in their place" to preserve their very

lives. We should not be surprised that, as a companion

legacy, some African Americans have been taught to be risk averse.

The early American innovation period of 1760-1830 involved introduction of coal steam power, the making and manipulation of metals for mechanical devices, and the invention of the cotton gin which led to growth in the textile industry. Innovation during this period began the slow move of US society away from an agrarian culture to an industrial one.

Of course, there were some African American innovators, even during this period, like Benjamin Banneker, who is not only credited with saving the design of Washington DC's layout, but who also predicted a solar eclipse, designed an irrigation system, designed watches, and other innovations. But he is not part of the face of science in America.

Those who were innovators, like Banneker, received little or no credit or income for their efforts. In general, while white Americans enjoyed increased wealth and prosperity because of innovation, black America did not. The same innovations that benefitted whites, sometimes caused further harm to African Americans. The innovations required increased labor from African Americans to, for example, pick more cotton. But blacks were not paid for the labor they performed. Those unpaid wages laid the foundation for black economic disenfranchisement.

The 1840-1870 innovation period featured increased mechanization of certain types of work previously performed manually and the formation of factories. During this timeframe, steel changed the design of farm implements and increased worker productivity. An example of this is the steel plow which replaced hoes in farming. In using the plow the speed in the preparation of farmland for planting greatly increased. Technology advancements continued to perfect the cotton gin. Railroads and the use of coal and steam power improved the transport of people and goods across the country. These innovations, often heralded in movies like the History Channel's *The Men Who Built America*, brought wealth to an increased number of white Americans. However, black Americans along with other citizens of color were often legally restricted from benefiting economically. Efforts by blacks to change this exclusion were often met with increased brutality and further limiting constraints.

While the Civil War, slave emancipation, and the start of Reconstruction occurred during this time, the African-American populace remained unable to take full advantage of the country's technological advances due to the impoverished state of its majority, the Black Codes of 1865 and 1866[ii] (laws that forbade their participation in entrepreneurial activities after the end of the Civil War), as well as laws that prevented education of blacks and fair compensation for their labor. Whites assisting blacks in entrepreneurial pursuits were also punished.

> *1. All contracts for labor made with freedmen, free*
> *negroes and mulattoes for a longer period than one*
> *month shall be in writing, and a duplicate, attested*
> *and read to said freedman, free negro or mulatto by*

*a beat, city or county officer, or two disinterested*

*white persons of the county in which the labor is to*

*performed, of which each party shall have one: and*

*said contracts shall be taken and held as entire*

*contracts, and if the laborer shall quit the service of*

*the employer before the expiration of his term of*

*service, without good cause, he shall forfeit his*

*wages for that year up to the time of quitting.*

*...Every civil officer shall, and every person may,*

*arrest and carry back to his or her legal employer*

*any freedman, free negro, or mulatto who shall have*

*quit the service of his or her employer before the*

*expiration of his or her term of service without good*

*cause; and said officer and person shall be entitled*

*to receive for arresting and carrying back every*

*deserting employee aforesaid the sum of five*

*dollars....*

*... If any person shall persuade or attempt to*

*persuade, entice, or cause any freedman, free negro*

*or mulatto to desert from the legal employment of
any person before the expiration of his or her term of
service, or shall knowingly employ any such
deserting freedman, free negro or mulatto, or shall
knowingly give or sell to any such deserting
freedman, free negro or mulatto, any food, raiment,
or other thing, he or she shall be guilty of a
misdemeanor....*

*3. All freedmen, free negroes and mulattoes in this
State, over the age of eighteen years, found on the
second Monday in January, 1866, or thereafter, with no
lawful employment or business, or found unlawful
assembling themselves together, either in the day or
night time, and all white persons assembling
themselves with freedmen, Free negroes or mulattoes,
or usually associating with freedmen, free negroes or
mulattoes, on terms of equality, or living in adultery or
fornication with a freed woman, freed negro or mulatto,
shall be deemed vagrants, and on conviction thereof*

*shall be fined in a sum not exceeding, in the case of a freedman, free negro or mulatto, fifty dollars, and a white man two hundred dollars, and imprisonment at the discretion of the court, the free negro not exceeding ten days, and the white man not exceeding six months….*(excerpt from the Mississippi Black Codes of 1865).

Again, despite dire circumstances, there were African American innovators. But, again, in general, innovation did not mean prosperity or emancipation for blacks. Most blacks were confined to being the labor which used the technology, if they had any access to the new inventions of the period. Though there was increased need for labor during this period of the Industrial Revolution, most black labor went unpaid. Black entrepreneurial spirit was dealt another crushing blow from the lack of capital.

The 1880-1900 period of innovation was the era of the railroads and the full transition of the US economy to an industrial-based society. During this timeframe in the US, technological innovations became more complex and sophisticated. Transportation advances grew beyond the nationwide introduction of railroads and railways to creation of the automobile and first airplanes. To power these new highly complex mechanical machines, the science of petroleum refinement became a new industry. Steam power and the discovery of electricity resulted in the push for engineering to develop hydroelectric power capability throughout the country. Contrary to previous innovation periods, African-Americans made limited inroads into the economic prosperity occurring because of the labor needs of these new industries. Greater access to education also allowed more blacks to become producers of innovations within this new societal construct. Examples of inventors during this time period are:

**Elijah McCoy** – recognized as a prolific inventor with over 50 patents, similar to Thomas Edison, for lubricating systems, some of which were used with steam locomotive engines. His work is the source of the saying "the real

McCoy"; clients sought out his superiorly designed oil lubricator system.

**Sarah E. Goode** – the second black woman awarded a patent. She received her award for the hideaway bed, later called the Murphy bed, in July of 1885.

**Granville T. Woods** – an electrical engineer who invented the Synchronous Multiplex Railway Telegraph, an invention enabling communications between moving trains and train depots. A court decision restored his rights as the inventor of the technology after Thomas Edison falsely claimed ownership.

**Lewis H. Latimer** – a draftsman who prepared Alexander Graham Bell's blueprints for his patent application. He oversaw many projects installing the first electric lights in building both in the US and Canada. He was awarded 8 patents and became the first Chief Draftsman of the General Electric/Westinghouse Board of Patent Control in 1896.

**Dr. Daniel Hale Williams** – an African American surgeon who performed the first open heart surgery on July 9, 1893.

However, serious limitations remained on these advancements due to Jim Crow laws, overt racism, and physical terrorism from the white majority. (A closer look at the white riots against the black community in 1920's Tulsa, Oklahoma, which is discussed later, provides a picture of the restrictions' magnitude.) These limitations have impacted blacks' economic advancement and their willingness to be innovators: being an innovator, a show-off, being "uppity" might cost one his or her life, and might even lead to the death of a community.

During this same period, millions of blacks were moving north as part of the Great Migration in order to gain economic opportunity in several manufacturing industries and in hopes of escaping violent racism. These industries did improve the economic conditions of some blacks. Yet none of these individuals actually would be able to attain enough economic wealth within the industries to start factories of their own that, for example, produced vehicles as part of the automotive technology race, or to own stockyards.

Innovation and advancements in agriculture and nutrition were fueling the growth of a new food industry. However, millions of black people who remained in the southern United States working as sharecroppers in the agriculture industry were forcefully kept from being a part of the food innovation wave. Blacks, instead, were relegated to being poorly paid laborers and consumers, and blocked from being co-leaders of the new industry. These emerging industries took advantage of black America's labor, but left America's black citizens with no wealth, many living in extreme poverty. Blacks who found success as innovators, like Annie Malone and Madame C.J. Walker, found success outside of mainstream industries.

Black men, who fought in World War I, selflessly served their country, and had been exposed to the introduction of advanced military technology. Many had also experienced some levels of equality while fighting in Europe, but came back to experience terror, violence, and racism at home. Rather than welcoming them into the technology race, the society they had served still treated them as inferior and unequal. Homes and businesses in the few prosperous black communities that had managed to acquire wealth, even despite significant hurdles, were decimated by financial and physical destruction of properties by whites. Race riots by whites against blacks seeking prosperity were numerous, reaching a fever pitch in 1919 (also known as "the Red Summer")[iii] and spread across the nation.

One episode of this violence—both physical and financial--occurred in the spring of 1921 in Oklahoma. Tulsa, "The Black Wall Street" most popularly known, was one of the wealthiest black communities in the nation. Drawn to the Oklahoma oil fields and the opportunity to work and achieve the American dream, black Tulsans had created a thriving community of schools, churches, businesses and homes. According to Linda Christensen, author of The Zinn Education Project's *Burning Tulsa: The Legacy of Dispossession*:

*The term "race riot" does not adequately describe the events of May 31—June 1, 1921 in Greenwood, a black neighborhood in Tulsa, Oklahoma. In fact, the term itself implies that both blacks and whites might be equally to blame for the lawlessness and violence. The historical record documents a sustained and murderous assault on black lives and property. This assault was met by a brave but unsuccessful armed defense of their community by some black World War I veterans and others.*

*During the night and day of the riot, deputized whites killed more than 300 African Americans. They looted and burned to the ground 40 square blocks of 1,265 African American homes, including hospitals, schools, and churches, and destroyed 150 businesses. White deputies and members of the National Guard arrested and detained 6,000 black Tulsans who were released only upon being vouched for by a white employer or other white citizen. Nine thousand African Americans were left homeless and lived in tents well into the*

*winter of 1921.*

Hundreds of blacks and 21 whites lost their lives during the race riot conducted by whites resulting in the burning and destruction of Black Wall Street. The loss of lives, property, and wealth sent a clear message to blacks: stay in your place. An effort to address riots and to pass anti-lynching laws[iv] in the US Congress, to mitigate this violence against African Americans and provide economic support, was politically stonewalled by white state and federal governments. This legislative failure only helped to legitimize and increase the occurrences of terroristic attacks by whites on their black neighbors.

Actions like these, attacks by angry white men on blacks working to build prosperous communities, happened across the country in places like Chicago. IL; East St. Louis, MO; Charleston, SC; Knoxville, TN; Tulsa, OK; and Washington, DC. The theme continued to echo: *stay in your place.* African Americans weren't welcomed in front doors, on the front seats of buses, and they weren't welcome in the doors of industry.

As one self-reliant antidote to this hostile and desperate 1920s environment, Marcus Garvey undertook the approach of attempting to lead African Americans to create their own industries and innovations. Garvey, "The Negro Moses", became powerful, infamous, and, to many whites, very dangerous as his efforts lead blacks toward the attainment of black wealth and economic prosperity. His Negro Factories Corporation (as part of the international Universal Negro Improvement Association) effort and the start of the Black Star Line movement (which encouraged blacks to create their own industries and expatriate themselves to Africa so that they could form a country of their own making) telegraphed the message that blacks could become an economic force in and of themselves. Garvey's message of self-sufficiency found more support overseas. His efforts to help blacks in the US was unsustainable.

Despite tragedies like the decimation of Black Wall Street, African-Americans continued to make some, but not widespread, advances in the STEM fields. The legacy of black innovation continued on.

**Dr. Sadie Tanner Mossell Alexander, Ph. D., J.D. -** became the first black woman to earn a PhD in the US for her work in economics along with being the first black woman to enter the Pennsylvania Bar. She was never able to work in the prosperous field of economics.

**George Washington Carver** - was the premiere black scientist of the day for his inventions associated with peanuts and his testimony before the US Congress in support of white peanut farmers and the peanut industry. However, many of his advancements never helped his fellow African Americans share in the ownership and wealth of the growing peanut industry.

**Bessie Coleman** - known more popularly as "Queen Bess", became one of aviation's few black faces during this period. She gained national and international acclaim through her notoriety as the first African American, male or female, to earn an aviation pilot's license in 1921. Queen Bess journeyed to France to earn her license due to rejection by American flight schools because of her race and gender. She traveled the country as a flying daredevil. While some African Americans became players in the avionics field, they were still locked out of positions as leaders and producers in the technological development of the industry.

Other blacks would follow Queen Bess' lead, like, years later, the renowned **Tuskegee Airmen**. According to their official history:

> In spite of adversity and limited opportunities, African Americans have played a significant role in U.S. military history over the past 300 years. They were denied military leadership roles and skilled training because many believed they lacked qualifications for combat duty. Before 1940, African Americans were barred from flying for the U.S. military. Civil rights organizations and the black press exerted pressure

*that resulted in the formation of an all-African-American pursuit squadron based in Tuskegee, Alabama, in 1941. They became known as the Tuskegee Airmen. "Tuskegee Airmen" refers to all who were involved in the so-called "Tuskegee Experience," the Army Air Corps program to train African Americans to fly and maintain combat aircraft. The Tuskegee Airmen included pilots, navigators, bombardiers, maintenance and support staff, instructors, and all the personnel who kept the planes in the air.*

*The military selected Tuskegee Institute to train pilots because of its commitment to aeronautical training. Tuskegee had the facilities, and engineering and technical instructors, as well as a climate for year round flying. The first Civilian Pilot Training Program students completed their instruction in May 1940. The Tuskegee program was then expanded and became the center for African-American aviation during World War II.*

The historic lack of opportunity, lack of recognition, and hostile reaction to black advancement is not peculiar to STEM and can be found across many areas of endeavor, including the arts, politics, and even some sports.

These three conditions - lack of opportunity, lack of recognition, and hostile reaction to black advancement - are related to the historical treatment of African Americans in the United States, and gains or lack of advancement in the area of Civil Rights. Their impact spreads throughout the fabric of the black experience and are often expressed in the arts. During the 1920s, even black artists experienced the effects of the turbulent period. They took the counter approach of developing their own art movement and called it the Harlem Renaissance. Often crossing color lines, a new crop of black writers, artists, poets, and artisans demonstrated that blacks could be producers of new artistic innovations. These innovations brought with them wealth and economic improvement unlike innovations in other parts of black society.

This combination of innovation and wealth generation by black artists continues today.

Like the Harlem Renaissance artists, individuals like surgeon Vivien Thomas, chemist Percy Julian, and Provident Hospital founder Dr. Daniel Hale Williams, achieved in STEM despite the odds. They did so because they had the courage to push back against those who would deny them opportunity, and against the widely-held notion that they should stay in their place. Their work in STEM also brought the rare outcome of economic opportunities to other African Americans.

Innovation has continued with the accelerated establishment of numerous STEM-related industries and products such as the transistor radio, food science, and pharmaceuticals among many others. This transition continued its acceleration into the 1950s and 60s with the age of the microprocessor, establishment of Silicon Valley, and the subsequent STEM-powered electronics industry.

The Civil Rights Movement that fought for voting rights, equal housing, and equal schools happening during this same time period was still occupied with basic black survival. Once again, African Americans were restricted from enjoying the fruits of the new innovation wave taking place.

In Greensboro, North Carolina, young college students had the courage to challenge the status quo. On February 1, 1960, roommates Joseph McNeil and Ezell Blair, Jr., Franklin McCain, and David Richmond, students at predominately black North Carolina Agricultural and Technical College, staged a sit-in at the local Woolworth's store lunch counter, a place reserved for whites only. Many of you reading this book may know this story well. My family has a proud connection to these young men and their efforts. A nephew attended the same college as the "A&T Four". Some of my family members participated in the sit-ins once the movement gained strength.

Over a week's time, the A&T Four were joined by more students and supporters who were confronted by angry white mobs who cursed and assaulted them in order to deter the blacks from seeking service at the lunch counters.

The idea of sit-ins rapidly spread to other students across the state. According to a Student Non-Violent Coordinating Committee (SNCC) history:

> *Over the next week, sit-ins occurred in the North Carolina cities of Winston-Salem, Durham, Raleigh, Charlotte, Fayetteville, High Point, Elizabeth City and Concord. On February 10, Hampton, Virginia became the first city outside of North Carolina to experience a sit-in, and by the end of the month, sit-ins had occurred in more than thirty communities in seven states. By the end of April, sit-ins had reached every southern state and attracted a total of perhaps as many as 50,000 students.*

> *Most of these sit-ins [which were joined by some white supporters] were characterized by strict discipline on the part of the protesters, minimizing physical assaults. However, several outbreaks of violence occurred when the protests involved high school students. The first of such events took place February 16, 1960, when*

*hundreds of black and white high school students*
*fought each other after a sit-in.*

*These sit-ins thrust black student leaders into the*
*spotlight, a position for which they were often*
*unprepared.*

To support the students, Ella Baker, of the Southern

Christian Leadership Conference, met with student leaders in

Raleigh at Shaw University on April 16, 1960 to begin training

and mentoring them. That meeting was the beginning of the

Student Non-violent Coordinating Committee (SNCC). While

Silicon Valley was in its early stages of bringing new wealth

and opportunity to white Americans, black Americans were

fighting for their basic rights. Black exclusion from the

economic benefits of a new technological revolution repeated

once again.

Innovation during the period of black Civil Rights

turmoil led to the age of the computer, the Internet (1990-

2000), and today's mobile device age. Although African-

Americans have benefited from the technologies, as have

other ethnic communities within the country, the benefits have been primarily those as innovation *consumers* rather than *producers*. Innovation does not correlate with social advancement: Some blacks who have been innovators have not been fully recognized. Others who received recognition often were unable to translate their achievements into broader economic success for the black collective at-large. Only the innovators, and not the consumers, benefit from sustainable economic prosperity on a widespread and intergenerational basis. This is the painful lesson African Americans must learn from our fragmented, suppressed, and unrecognized technology leadership in this nation.

## Looking to the future

There is hope. Though, in the past, they have not received the notoriety afforded their white counterparts, and against overwhelming odds, there are black STEM heroes upon whose shoulders we can build a different future in this new technology age.

**Katherine G. Johnson**  - NASA mathematician who calculated, among many other computations, the trajectory for the space flight of Alan Shepard, the first American in space; John Glenn, the first American to orbit earth; and Apollo 11, the first human mission to the moon. She is still sought out today as an inspirational speaker to young blacks going into the aerospace field. One of her daughters, a recent acquaintance, is an alumna of my father's alma mater, Hampton University, which is a historically black college and university renowned for its work with NASA.

**Mark Dean** - co-inventor of the personal computer, which dramatically changed the way people work and play. He continues to teach and train young black computer science and electrical engineers at the University of Tennessee.

**Dr. Patricia Bath** - In 1981, Bath invented the Laserphaco Probe, which she continued to perfect and later patented in 1988. The tool was used during eye surgery to correct cataracts. She was the first African American to complete a residency in ophthalmology; the first woman to chair an ophthalmology residency program in the United States; and the first African American female doctor to secure a medical patent. She also co-founded the American Institute for the Prevention of Blindness. Dr. Bath continues to inspire new generations of blacks interested in medical careers.

**Lonnie G. Johnson** – multi-millionaire Johnson began working as an engineer for NASA's Jet Propulsion Laboratory in 1979. During his time at NASA, Johnson worked on the Galileo mission to Jupiter, the Mars Observer project, and the Cassini mission to Saturn. He earned multiple awards from NASA for his spacecraft control systems. But Johnson is possibly best known for inventing the Super Soaker water gun. He successfully sued Hasbro for almost $73 million in royalties that the toy company had failed to pay on his inventions. Mr. Johnson and his companies provide an example of the business achievements available to young black STEM entrepreneurs.

**James E. West** - In 1957, West went to work at Bell Labs. He and fellow scientist Gerhard M. Sessler developed an inexpensive, compact, and highly sensitive microphone, which they patented in 1962. Today, 90 percent of microphones use their technology, including those in cell phones, laptops, baby monitors, and hearing aids. Through his efforts, African Americans have career, mentorship, and scholarship opportunities with Bell Labs, a major international research and innovation company. He is changing the future of blacks in his area of STEM for the better.

Like these black STEM achievers, there are black achievers in other fields, like writer Toni Morrison, tennis great Serena Williams, musician John Legend, and Barak Obama who have refused to limit themselves to the place that others would assign them. The future is full of hope as we consider the possibilities that lie ahead, but only if black Americans learn from the past and act.

People of color in all parts of the world—like the Middle East, China, India, and South Africa—are joining the technology race and are making significant strides. Nevertheless, there remains a shortage of trained and qualified individuals to take advantage of the world's technological growth. According to the National Math and Science Initiative, the U.S. may be short as many as three million high-skilled workers by 2018.

What is needed is a corps of black achievers, particularly black STEM achievers—the young, the displaced, the disenfranchised—who are willing to pick up the mantle of those who have gone before them. These black STEM achievers must possess the courage, confidence, and support necessary to make and demand a place for themselves at the global counter of technology.

# Chapter 3:
# It's A STEM STEM STEM STEM World

*"So much technology, so little talent."*

~Victor Vinge
Author and former Professor of Mathematics
San Diego State University

In the early 1960s, United Artist Films released the movie "It's A Mad Mad Mad Mad World"[v]. The dramedy (i.e. a drama and comedy) tells the story of a disparate group of individuals in a chaotic and frenetic race. Their goal is to be the first to find and claim the buried treasure of money left behind by a dying driver. They become involuntary participants in a massive traffic jam. As the film progresses, the characters employ increasingly outrageous tactics and modern technology to reach the treasure.

Today's world is equally as chaotic and frenetic as the Mad Mad Mad Mad World movie. Technology has turned the world upside down, and brought humankind to a fast and furious quest to profit from its treasures. Examples of this can

74

be found everywhere. Apple, the largest US technology company and maker of the iPhone, iPad, and Mac computer products, races to release new versions of its products every 8-12 months. Google, another large US technology company overseen by the Alphabet, Inc. conglomerate[vi], is perfecting the driverless car and working to stretch the boundaries of computer technology design in automotive design. Tesla Motors, a highly regarded advanced technology company new to the automotive industry, is successfully increasing the market for electric vehicles, generating incredible market value, and leading advanced technology efforts in the battery and aerospace industries. IBM and General Electric, two older global technology companies that have been in place for over 100 years, along with numerous other companies and new startups, are bringing new and highly profitable information technology-related products to the healthcare industry on a daily basis. Oil companies, such as BP, Shell, and Duke Energy, are leading efforts to identify petroleum-alternative energy sources by embracing biofuel technology. First Solar, the largest solar energy generating company in the US, is leading the new technology industry into accelerated growth.

Traditional media outlets such as CBS, ABC, and NBC,

upended by cable media in the 1980s and 1990s, are all now

threatened again by new Internet-based companies like

Netflix and Hulu that have become major competitors in the

entertainment industry. Banks and banking institutions are

rapidly expanding their technology platter by introducing

mobile and bitcoin-like technology to their online (i.e. Internet-

based) financial industry. Entrepreneurs have also joined the

technology race. According to Forbes magazine, there was

one technology startup beginning in the US every two days

(i.e. 48 hours) in 2013. The technology race is affecting life

around the planet. Countries that once struggled economically

are beginning to turn their fortunes around by encouraging

and supporting the development of new technology. Asia and

Africa, for example, are growing financially due to the

technology expansions taking place within their continents.

Many Americans, including black Americans, lack an

understanding of this change in the world. They have not and

are not preparing themselves to prosper in this new

worldview. They are missing from the frenzied competition. This is a significant black STEM problem.

As the technology race continues to accelerate, global concerns increase that there are not enough qualified people trained in STEM-related fields to work in these new and newly morphing companies. In 2011, the international Organisation for Economic Co-operation and Development (i.e. the OECD), whose mission is to help governments create conditions for economic prosperity while also fighting poverty, issued a report entitled, "A Skilled Workforce for Strong, Sustainable, and Balanced Growth"[vii]. The report outlined the need for increased technical (i.e. STEM) training of the world's workforce to meet the needs of rapid innovation occurring in developed, developing and emerging countries. The US, and its workforce, was cited as a country that may not be prepared to meet its future training and workforce needs.

The lack of widespread STEM-related capabilities within the US workforce has received a great deal of attention recently. Several departments and agencies, such as the US

Department of Labor, with its report entitled "Futurework –

Trends and Challenges for Work in the 21$^{st}$ Century"[viii], have

issued documents explaining the technology workforce crisis

and its impact on America's future.

President Obama has been dubbed the first

"Commander in Chief of Technology" for sounding the alarm

concerning the need for more STEM capabilities. In a speech

given to the National Academies of Science, President

Obama walked the audience through a litany of statistics

indicating that the US was falling behind other developed

nations in the areas of STEM. He emphasized that there was

a need to get America back on track. "Science is more

essential for our prosperity, our security, our health, our

environment, and our quality of life than it has ever been. And

if there was ever a day that reminded us of our shared stake

in science and research, it's today."[ix] He went on to say the

following,

*"I believe it is not in our American character to follow – but to lead. And it is time for us to lead once again. I am here today to set this goal: we will devote more than three percent of our GDP to research and development. We will not just meet, but we will exceed the level achieved at the height of the Space Race, through policies that invest in basic and applied research, create new incentives for private innovation, promote breakthroughs in energy and medicine, and improve education in math and science. This represents the largest commitment to scientific research and innovation in American history."*

Since that event, the federal government has worked to fund innovation activities throughout the country, implement policies that increase the number of young people being educated about STEM, and inform the American public of the need for every citizen to improve his and her math and science capabilities. The President's Council of Advisors on Science and Technology (PCAST) and the Office of Science and Technology Policy (OSTP) have also released a series of pivotal reports highlighting the extent of the STEM talent pool problem and the recommended steps needed to improve America's STEM workforce deficiencies.

The United States is at an important crossroads in the technological advancement of its people. The African American community is at an even more critical juncture.

Wealth and prosperity for Black Americans can no longer be wholly dependent upon the economic "levers" of the past. Attaining widespread middle class status through the employment of physical labor in industries such as automobile manufacturing is a thing of the past. Geographical relocation to find better jobs, as was accomplished through the Great Migration, is ceasing. The 21$^{st}$ century no longer needs masses of people trained with vocational or labor skills. As the world moves toward a knowledge-based economy, professional jobs in areas like automobile manufacturing are rapidly diminishing. Affirmative action initiatives net fewer and fewer opportunities to obtain well-paying jobs at the federal, state, and local governmental level. Opportunities in professions like education, law, and public policy are decreasing. These levers were successful at improving African American economic positions during the boom of the post-World War eras, and during the Civil Rights Movement of the 1960's and 70's when blacks were shut out of the technology revolutions taking place. Today's situation is radically different.

As a result, African American economic advancement has become stagnant and the upward mobility gained one to two generations ago is quickly being lost. Black unemployment levels remain double that of other ethnic groups in the country.

Economic inequality has become an equal opportunity issue for all Americans, but especially for black Americans. The inequality phenomenon experienced by a growing number of Americans is a reflection of the United States' transformation into a knowledge-based society. In the knowledge-based world, innovators in the fields of STEM are acquiring and accumulating large portions of the country's wealth. Numerous new governmental and grassroots efforts have been started to encourage all Americans, including the African American public, to become knowledge workers in this new society. Historical restrictions against African Americans in all areas of technology development are being lifted. As stated earlier, these efforts have yet to result in great advances and opportunities for STEM within a majority of black circles.

Despite focused efforts by small business programs to encourage African American entrepreneurs to start technology companies, black technology entrepreneurs continue to be a small portion of the total number of US entrepreneurs kicking off technology companies. Though there are federal efforts to help identify and target the increase of young black children into STEM academic tracks throughout K-12, the total number of black high school students that graduate and go on to pursue STEM studies in college remains low.

And despite propaganda indicating that African-Americans trained in STEM do not exist, there are black people trained in STEM—*unemployed* black people. Corporate outreach efforts to attract such candidates still fall short of providing gainful employment to all *existing* qualified black candidates in America. Growth in the number of H1B visas, the tech world's answer to gaining more workers for unfilled jobs, only worsens the outlook for unemployed STEM-trained blacks[x].

## Winning at the Game

Still, we should not be discouraged. In Malcolm
Gladwell's book, "David and Goliath: Underdogs, Misfits, and
the Art of Battling Giants", the author presents the idea that
great successes can be achieved by underdogs. He defines
underdogs as those individuals who do not seem to possess
the resources that others have and, yet, find a creative way to
command the resources at their disposal in such a way to
execute a winning outcome[xi]. To support his premise,
Gladwell presents a detailed analysis of the fight between two
individuals of the Bible; Goliath, a seasoned warrior of gigantic
physical size who appears to out-armor and outman a small
young shepherd boy named David dressed as such and with
no war experience. But when the fight between the two
begins, it is David who wins. Gladwell surmises that this
surprising turn of events can be attributed to David's inherent
realization of one thing about himself – his disadvantages are
*really* his advantages. And so it must be with the black
community when it considers its current apparent

shortcomings with regards to the technological shift occurring in the world. Black Americans are David and the technology world is their Goliath. However, rather than destroying or overtaking the technology world, black Americans achieve by first identifying its disadvantages. These disadvantages include insufficient technology designs and lack of technology features meeting the needs of a diverse customer base. Once these disadvantages are acknowledged and understood then the community must turn them into their underdog advantages. For example, African Americans might be prime candidates for jobs testing new products and new systems, offering advice to companies on their products' consumer interface in urban settings or with non-mainstream use cases. African Americans might be better at finding and encouraging black startups and at serving as recruiters for companies with diversity initiatives.

This book hopes to begin that comprehensive thought process by suggesting ways in which we, the black community, and those around us can think more deeply and differently about building our prowess in modern society. It's time for us to become a prosperous David in a globally competitive and technological Goliath-like world. Those with STEM skills and capabilities are leading the race and black Americans must get in the race. We must join the chaotic race. It's a STEM STEM STEM STEM World, baby!

# Chapter 4:
# Birthing a Nation of STEM Achievers

*"The problem with our education system is not that parents do not have a choice. The problem is that inequities continue to exist."*

~Patsy Mink, Former US Congresswoman

"I'm just not good at school work, Aunt Cynthia", my nephew would often tell me. "Not everyone is smart enough to go to college and get a degree in science like you. Some of us just don't get science. We didn't get it when we were kids in grade school and we still don't get it now that we're adults." I saw his disappointment as he looked away. Inside I grew angry thinking about the unfairness of an educational system that left him and other young black youths feeling this way.

STEM training is not for the faint of heart. It's tough. But blacks, as a people, have never shied away from hard work. Many African-American experts believe that the decline of the community begins and ends with a lack of equity in education and inadequate early career guidance. This results in home conditions deficient in STEM. This is not acceptable.

My own father was a graduate of a technical program at Hampton University in Virginia. He impressed upon me very early in life that education was important. While his own dreams of being an engineer were interrupted by early marriage and family, he began feeding that dream to me in my earliest years. A Microsoft-commissioned study by Harris Interactive showed that parents play a significant role in driving their child's STEM interest[xii]. I was lucky my parents encouraged taking STEM classes when I was a child. However, many children aren't blessed with parents or role models interested in STEM.

Reinforcement of this troublesome non-STEM worldview takes place, in many cases, before a young black child enters a K-12 educational system. Young children that do not present a mastery of basic science and math skills by the seventh grade are typically lost forever from entering the STEM world[xiii].

Starting at the beginning of life, a majority of African-Americans are born into environments where STEM-related family activities and early education do not exist. An earlier chapter provides historical context for this shortcoming. This lack of existence is generational and cemented from change by the poverty experienced by numerous black families across the country. Many urban black communities are devoid of role models who are part of the STEM world because these individuals are living in other communities. Daily battles to survive in poverty-ridden living conditions overshadow thoughts of succeeding in a technology-based world. The mindset and worldview that includes STEM aspirations is missing right at the beginning of a new black life.

A non-STEM emphasis takes place not only in many black homes, but also, in many cases, when a young black child enters a K-12 educational system. For a growing number of black youth, their schools suffer from tumultuous budget, personnel, and operational friction. This chaos complicates teaching children necessary skills in STEM. Schools with large African-American student bodies have become the playgrounds of America's "lab rat experiments"; continual testing grounds for new ways of staffing (e.g. Teach for America), new ways of operating (e.g. charter schools), and new ways of teaching (e.g. Common Core). While STEM-related class activities may be part of these various changes, the students still struggle with limited exposure to the STEM fields once they leave the schoolhouse doors. Students return to homes where STEM lessons are unsupported by their parents leading them to return to the pursuit of liberal arts and sports programs as their major focus.

This cycle of STEM deprivation can continue into the college years for African-Americans fortunate enough to enter college. With inadequate STEM foundations from their K-12 experience, young blacks enter college usually pursuing non-STEM studies[xiv]. If they do pursue STEM fields of study, they are often without role models to help mentor them successfully through the program because there are few minorities in STEM faculty positions[xv]. Because of this deficiency, blacks that enter college seeking STEM degrees often transfer to other fields of study or do not graduate from the collegiate system. Of those students that do graduate successfully, few pursue advanced graduate and post-graduate degrees in technology[xvi].

It's easier to replicate something you've already seen.

Additionally, the lack of family STEM role models is worsened by a lack of neighborhood role models. Many urban black communities are devoid of role models who are part of the STEM world because those who might be role models have chosen to live in other more affluent communities. There are very few images of successful African Americans reflected in the media. Fortunately or unfortunately, TV often tells us who we are and who we can become. The successful African American role models that TV presents are sports figures, entertainers, and, sometimes, Blacks who have done well in other liberal arts arenas. The images tell African American children that "smart" and "tech" don't equate with Black people, not on TV—just watch *The Big Bang Theory*[xvii]—and not in the world.

Given all of this, it's fair to say that birthing a generation of black STEM lovers goes against uncertain odds when considering the numerous complications faced. But, once again, there is hope.

It is often when faced with seemingly insurmountable state of affairs that solutions can seem illusive and elude us. When deep into the details of a problem, it is hard to see the forest for the trees and looking at the forest is sometimes where we need to be. However, there are pockets of individuals and activities occurring around the country, that if brought together into one collective effort would significantly advance Black America's foray into the advanced technologies and create increased wealth for the entire community.

There are numerous individual grassroots activities to increase African American interest in the STEM fields. Expectations are that these efforts will culminate into a significant uptake of black interest in technology. Many of

these efforts are in the academic arena and address issues

along the entire education continuum; pre-school, K-12,

college, graduate, post-graduate, and professional. From

formalized and highly inventive efforts, such as The Black

Family Technology Awareness Association located in Kansas

City whose mission is to close the technology gap between

black families and technology, Pittsburgh's TeckStart Day

Care (a black STEM-focused day care for children 3-13 years

of age), and the Technology Access Foundation (which

provides STEM education to low-income students in the

Greater Seattle area) to the highly formalized initiatives

spurred by support from the federal government, K-12 training

efforts are growing on a continuous basis. Call them the

"Freedom Schools of the 21$^{st}$ Century"; the programs are

numerous and prolific in all geographic locations around the

country. For a list of some of these programs and others

working to increase black success in STEM, visit

www.blackstemusa.com.

The individual programs are commendable, but a broader approach is necessary if we are to achieve widespread results. Communities, organizations like the NAACP and Urban League, and even black church denominations should begin to evaluate programs and institute viable ones. Black parents and community leaders who show up for school board and local government meetings have the power to demand that better STEM training and counseling be provided in local schools. Parents in cities like Chicago, Illinois[xviii]; Newark, NJ[xix]; Berkeley, California[xx]; Charleston, SC[xxi]; and in other locations have begun to make these requests with mixed results. Uniting these parents together under one STEM banner, as was done in the Civil Rights movement when attacking the issue of separate and unequal education, has a chance of getting change faster for black youth in every corner of the country.

Organizations like the Urban League and the NAACP (which already has in place the ACT-SO program--the NAACP's Afro-Academic, Cultural, Technological and

Scientific Olympics, a yearlong achievement program designed to recruit, stimulate, and encourage high academic and cultural achievement among African-American high school students) should more aggressively promote their efforts in black and mainstream media, both at the local and national level. Working together, they should create an organization-wide program that offers STEM advice and tutoring to black students and families throughout their lives.

Churches, which have long been the hub of support and advancement in the black economic community, should institute STEM training programs across their denominations. They might apply for grants, for example, to help support a Saturday tutoring/mentoring program. Church members themselves should also model leadership behaviors in STEM by becoming trained and knowledgeable of the latest technologies and their usage in their organizations.

This is a critical Civil Rights issue, and like SCLC's Ella Baker, pastors and youth leaders should institute training and coaching programs that meet weekly to mentor and tutor students and their parents. Not only do STEM students need training, they will also need support. They will have to be mentored in how to survive in an educational system that is sometimes hostile to African Americans who want to learn about STEM. The United Methodist Church's Black College Fund has such a program in its STEM partnership efforts with historically black colleges and universities (HBCUs). They conduct a Saturday STEM Academy with mentors to help young black youth prepare for college. Another program in Texas, the Austin Pre-Freshman Engineering Summer Program[xxii], offers an opportunity to prepare black youth for the rigors of the collegiate environment they will face.

There needs to be an effort to build a black STEM mindset with parents. As referenced earlier, research has found that if parents are college-educated, their children most often follow the path their parents have paved into the liberal arts, humanities, or STEM[xxiii]. If not, then their children follow the "survival path" or follow what they see on TV: embracing sports programs, entertainment, or other means of earning a living as their major focus or "way out." Pastors and community leaders can increase the probability of youth going into STEM through strategic alliances with parents, especially those who are college educated and STEM professionals. If a church-parental alliance existed, how might it work?

Many of the non-STEM worldview problems require systemic responses. However, a portion of the problems can be solved with a "quick fix." Let's examine one quick fix involving churches and black parents. The National Math and Science Initiative reports that:

- 44 percent of 2013 U.S. high school graduates are ready for college-level math.

- 36 percent of 2013 U.S. high school students are ready for college-level science.

- 26 percent of 2009 U.S. students took Algebra I before high school. (Up from 20 percent in 2005)

However, only 12 percent of black students and 17 percent of Hispanic students took Algebra I before high school in 2009.

Conversely, 48 percent of Asian students took Algebra I before high school in 2009. This is an issue ripe for a quick fix.

Because of budget constraints, there are fewer and fewer guidance counselors in public school; in some communities, two or more schools share one guidance counselor so that there is no one to advise students about what courses they should take. If, for example, each August, pastors addressed their congregations about the importance of students being prepared for college and challenged their young people to take Algebra I in middle school and Algebra II in high school, statistics about black students and math could be changed drastically. Black students' preparedness for college math would be drastically improved. Call it the "August Math Challenge." This is an example of an immediate action a church-parental STEM alliance could easily implement.

Talented African American youth are also targeted towards other areas of study because they, or others, don't believe they're capable. It's just not on "the radar screen." A STEM student related, "My family, because of my father's job, had relocated to Pennsylvania temporarily. When I went to the middle school the first day, the counselor had my school records and test scores. He seemed like a friendly, well-meaning guy, kind of a hippie with a long ponytail. He commended me on my grades and test scores. Then he said, 'I'll assign you to the B Track. I think you'll be happier there.' I objected immediately—it was probably mostly ego. I was college-bound and I'd always been in the highest track. The idea of B Track was off-putting: I had the grades to support being in A Track. He apologized. I think he was more worried about my social life than my education. I only knew of one black boy in A Track; I was the only girl."

Black students need to be mentored in asserting their needs and in sharing negative incidents with their families and churches, who can advocate for them. Church and parental alliances can help them.

Birthing generations of black STEMmers is not only a concern for parents, churches, and the community. It should be a concern for business. White corporations, like Google and Facebook, who are investing dollars in scholarships, should work to protect their investments by partnering with the other four constituent groups. Money is wonderful, but corporations must also mentor and provide advocates who can help the students navigate sometimes treacherous educational waters. Black mentorship and advocacy should continue throughout a talented black STEMmers life. Just as professional sports teams, like in the NBA, begin identifying and tracking talented students in middle school for recruitment when their professional career begins, tech companies must begin to do the same. Corporations must begin introducing students to the competitive STEM culture—support sports teams, provide fun and challenging summer camps—and take advantage of the opportunity to begin embracing the students' cultures in a symbiotic relationship that continues until professional employment. Invest face to face and for the long term.

Collegiate institutions also have a more formalized role to play. They must provide meaningful support for black college students who pursue STEM fields of study. African Americans entering college are often not equipped to navigate hostile educational waters, are often unprepared to encounter educational systems that do not support them, or that may even be, intentionally or unintentionally, adverse to their success. This can be overwhelmingly stressful in competitive academic programs. Sometimes, white male dominated STEM education, particularly at predominantly white institutions (PWI), is often exclusionary and elitist. This hostile atmosphere should be acknowledged by colleges. Measures to deal with this, such as required annual cultural competency training for faculty and staff, could help.

"It was culture shock. No one looked like me. I was the only African American female in a sea of over 700 engineering students, virtually all white male. The professor who addressed us said, 'Look to the right of you and then to the left. By the end of the semester, two of you will be gone.' I had been one of the top scholars at my school. It shook my confidence. I was intimidated."

These kinds of archaic educational strategies at colleges won't help America meet its STEM goals. Instead, these exclusionary strategies discourage talented students who are too young to have developed skills to cope and fight for themselves.

Additionally, black students are often without role models to help mentor them successfully through the program and culture because there are few minorities in STEM faculty positions[xxiv]. College faculty, staff, and student campus organizations, of all races, should implement formalized programs to enable African American students to build strong peer networks, with all races, as a form of STEM mentorship to prevent their derailment. This is important at all academic institutions, however it is critical for black youth in STEM programs at PWIs.

An acquaintance of mine related, "I planned to major in Engineering at the University of Illinois, but some of the professors actually seemed resentful of my presence, as though they assumed that I was incapable and didn't deserve to be there. I was a National Merit scholar, but I think they made other assumptions, perhaps, because of my race and gender. When I sought help, I was rebuffed. I wasn't prepared for the resentment; I came expecting an open, welcoming education. There were no African Americans, not even working as counselors, which I could go to for encouragement or advice. He didn't suggest resources, like tutors. I left. I'm sure none of my white male counterparts knew how I was being treated or what I was suffering. It probably looked to them like I wasn't qualified and just couldn't cut it."

My experience in attending a PWI for college is that it is a mixed blessing. I have attended two such schools, Kettering University and Cornell University. Both were excellent schools; top schools in their categories. I believed having the names of these schools as part of my academic credentials would open doors for me in some circles. I believed it would give me the benefit of the doubt when people met me; proof that I am smarter and more talented than "how I look." The "how I look" comment was an off-hand statement made to me during both of my academic experiences. I took the comment to mean that no one expected much from me since I was an ordinary looking dark-skinned black girl. I believed attending these prestigious schools would help rid people of that thought.

Going to a PWI was exciting and stressful at the same time. I felt that I had achieved a great accomplishment. I also garnered respect and enthusiasm from my family, friends, teachers, and church members who were excited that I was attending these top schools. Initially, I thought people of all races would look at and engage with me differently when they learned of my academic prowess simply through my association with storied institutions. It was a great and awesome feeling.

On the other side of the coin, going to PWIs for my academic training brought about two of the loneliest and sometimes most depressing periods of my life. I often felt that the student culture required that black students take a back seat to the white students. As a result, I sometimes felt I was battling the world alone during my academic experiences. Although many people who were in the academic environment often said they were blind to people's appearances and only cared about their skills and talents, I never found that to be true. A person's appearance (i.e. race and gender) directly impacts the way in which others will react to them. Biased responses to a young black person because of their appearance, whether intended or unintended, can often lead to an internalized negative response inside that person. For me, the negative response was an increased sense of separation from my peers and loneliness. Also, I was a victim of their sexual passes and rude sexual innuendoes—just another form of intimidation perhaps heightened because of my race. For self-protection, I would sometimes isolate myself even further from my peers. This was another cause of my loneliness.

The depressing part of going to a predominantly white institution (PWI) is that no matter how hard you work, there is always someone, either a fellow student or a narrow-minded professor, actively working to undermine your efforts. While most people are supportive of having people of diverse backgrounds in their midst, there are the vocal few who make things as difficult as they possibly can. Luckily, I found a way around this. When I was at Kettering, I joined a white sorority rather than a black sorority on campus. I will forever be grateful to these women for accepting me into their organization and helping advise me on the best way to make it through my undergraduate engineering program. These wonderful young women helped me overcome the racially-based aggressions, now called "microaggressions", I faced while in school.

Others, like the following STEM graduate, have different experiences attending PWIs. "I attended a historically black college for undergrad. But I went to grad school at a PWI. I felt invisible, isolated, ignored, and unimportant. It was as if didn't exist. I learned after the fact about study groups and gatherings even among people who shared an office with me. I didn't start getting invited until other students realized how well I was doing. I knew more people outside of my department than inside—was involved in the grad dorm and graduate student council. Other departments at my school did better at creating a welcoming environment than mine; others did worse (Math). Of course this was over 20 years ago so things may have changed."

It is important for collegiate African-Americans pursuing STEM degrees to realize that there are pros and cons to attending PWIs as there are with any other institution they are considering. Aggression and ostracism can take place even in STEM programs. Rather than letting students deal with these experiences alone, academic institutions should offer formalized training to their African American students in methods of building a strong network of peers. Supportive networks will help them get through difficult times. Well-advertised access to private counseling, if needed, could also help. All of these steps are important for producing a sustainable pipeline of black STEMmers.

It is also important for African American college students to understand the culture of the local environment where you are getting your education. This has a major influence on academic institutions. For example, southeastern Michigan, where Kettering is located, was primarily a blue collar area when I attended school. Many of the workers lived middle income lives on high school educations due to the salaries they were making in the manufacturing plants. The communities in this part of Michigan were also heavily segregated. While workers of different races interacted with each other from 7am-7pm, the rest of the time the races were separate. This made the atmosphere at school carry an undertone of slight racial division. On the other hand Ithaca, where I attended Cornell University for my graduate studies, was surrounded by one of the most Democratically-progressive communities in upstate New York. The student body was more ethnically and culturally diverse than the one at Kettering. A greater number of students came from upper class families. My classmates and I socialized primarily with the faculty and administrative staff. Many of these individuals were highly regarded academics in their fields. While I experienced racial hostility on the campus, there was no continuous undertone of tension as there had been at Kettering. Overall the faculty and administrative staff worked diligently to improve race relations. Racial hostilities, which still occurred, were publicly discouraged by the entire campus. I believe that this intolerance of racial strife was a reflection of the inclusive atmosphere that surrounded the college. Therefore a supportive local community for black STEMmers is also required.

As an African-American at a more inclusive PWI, you have to gird and steel yourself for the unfair actions that can be taken by the individuals in power around you. I remember being in an economics class at Cornell University in which the professor was not sympathetic in his classroom comments about the students that were struggling to make good grades in the class. Without naming anyone, he spent most of this time talking about how these students really should consider dropping the class because it was obvious to him that they would not be able to get passing grades. He heralded the students that were doing well in his class. I was one of the students he was discussing, one of the ones who were struggling. He didn't mention tutoring, but I learned that there were tutors on campus to help students with this class. I began to attend the tutoring sessions to prove the professor wrong: I wasn't stupid and would grasp the economics material as well as the other students he preferred. It wasn't until I arrived at the tutoring session that I learned that almost all of the people of color (which also included Asians) were together in the tutoring session. We were my professors "undesirable" group of students; the ones that he publicly belittled in his class and encouraged to quit. While I was disappointed that I was in this group, I was thankful for the opportunity to be taught the material and have a shot at passing the class. All of the students being tutored felt similarly. As a group, we banded together helping each other learn the class and tutorial materials. We were determined that none of us would fail the course. So when our grades began to increase on the subsequent homework assignments and tests, the antagonistic professor was caught off his guard. So much so, that he announced to the class that he thought some students who had been previously struggling were doing so well that he was sure they were cheating. As a result of his suspicion, he said that he would be making the classwork and tests even harder. It was obvious that this instructor harbored deep racial hatred issues that were going unchecked at the University.

None of us reported him because once you file an official complaint, then the burden of proof is not on the offender but on the offended. The effort spent proving our case might have compromised our other studies. Our relationships with the faculty and staff might be ruined. So even though the classwork got unfairly harder, none of the students in the tutoring group complained. We just put our heads even further to the grindstone and worked even harder. I am happy to report that all of us in the little economics class tutoring group passed the class with flying colors. We proved the racist professor wrong.

When attending a PWI, be aware that racial hatred can take many forms. It can be discouraging and it can cause you a great deal of difficulty. However, know that if you are admitted to a PWI, you possess the skills to succeed. Remember the Greensboro sit-ins; don't allow the open mental harassment that you may receive from the faculty to stop you. Use all the resources around you to support you in your endeavor. There are others that will help.

Predominantly white institutions also have an important role to play in helping black students in STEM programs. Faculty and staff of all races should offer to become mentors of their African American students. Black students should be encouraged to attend networking events. Supportive peers and faculty can help them survive the cultural and racially-charged issues they may face. As I and others found in our collegiate experiences at PWIs, having a strong network of supporters, no matter their race or role, can help a person succeed without feeling sad and alone. If you can help a black student through these troubled times, it is all that matters.

During all this, it must be said, I neglected the faith that had been my foundation. It was this same faith that restored me and always gave me hope during my darkest hours.

Given the stories and experiences shared, solutions to improving the collegiate experience of African American students in STEM should include these summarized strategies:

- Universities must make it a priority to encourage and hire faculty sensitive and committed to the identification and development of STEM trained African American scholars. It should be part of the faculty review process.

- Endow professors who specialize in STEM and in supporting black STEM achievers. Encourage unendowed professors to help mentor these students.

- Institutions of higher learning must evaluate their STEM curriculums to make certain that what is taught is necessary and not exclusionary.

113

- Students must be assertive about making sure their needs are met. They must find the courage to speak up about educators who treat them unfairly and refuse to be turned away from the STEM lunch counter.

- Students must strive to build strong networks with peers of all backgrounds. Others may face similar hostilities and provide alternative strategies that can help.

- Because students have greater opportunity to achieve through STEM, parents must be supportive of their children's STEM efforts. Cheer them on. Look for opportunities to expose them to STEM-related activities like NAACP's ACT-SO competition and the Tuskegee Airmen's STEM camp.

- Parents, churches, and black community leaders must push for the inclusion of information about Africa in world history classes and about black STEM heroes (more than George Washington Carver) so that black students have STEM role models. History and education devoid of Africans and blacks perpetuates a sort of intellectual, economic, emotional, and cultural violence.

- Churches should develop outreach programs to support local STEM college students and to help them survive grueling study schedules and culture shock.

- The media also has a part to play. Bill Cosby's Dr. Huxtable, from the 1980s sitcom, was one of the last STEM achievers shown to be accomplished, well-off, and cool[xxv]. What most children are exposed to are images of entertainers and athletes, many of whom are questionable role models. Because this is a national crisis, a PR campaign should be instituted, like the anti-smoking public service announcements, that feature African Americans and promote intelligence and STEM as the "new sexy." Black and white media must develop programs that feature intelligent black STEMmers, much like The Big Bang Theory[xxvi]. An

115

example is the African American-focused episode of the "We the Geeks", a Whitehouse Google+ Hangout series[xxvii].

- A touring Black STEM Heroes Corps should be developed so that students can see, feel, and hear from STEM heroes who look like them and who are interested in their success.

As an alternative, if PWI institutions of higher learning do not respond to the needs of black STEM students, then organizations like the Congressional Black Caucus, the NAACP, the Urban League, Al Sharpton's National Action Network, and the Rainbow Coalition, must work to employ a lesson from black STEM pioneers like Bessie Coleman. They must build partnerships with foreign universities and nations, like China and India, where African Americans can train to earn STEM degrees. This kind of effort will require training in foreign languages but might ultimately give black STEM-trained students an advantage when seeking employment here and in foreign countries. The ultimate goal is to increase black presence in STEM. It may be achievable with this out-of-the-box strategy.

There is yet another excellent, though sometimes overlooked and undervalued, source for STEM training right in front of us.

PWIs are not the only STEM training option. Many Black STEM heroes and inventors, like Dr. Patricia Bath and Lonnie Johnson, were trained at historically black colleges (HBCUs). Not only do HBCUs turn out highly competent STEM graduates, they also turn out highly confident graduates. Confidence is integral to life-long success.

A student in North Carolina Central University's BRITE program, shared, "The professors really care. And the undergrad students here are doing things that students have to wait until grad school to do at other North Carolina schools." BRITE (Biomanufacturing Research Institute and Technology Enterprise) is "one of the newest and most innovative biotechnology educational initiatives in the country and the only formal biotech degree program offered by a North Carolina university."

Other HBCU graduates share similar experiences. "For undergrad I went to Johnson C. Smith in Charlotte. I was fortunate enough to find a faculty member to mentor me very early and worked on her research project for four years. She guided me in not only research training and experiences but also in what classes I needed on my transcript to look good to graduate schools. She tried to make sure I had comparable experiences as students attending larger institutions."

Another shared, "My professors cared and wanted to make sure that my education was rigorous enough that I could survive the challenges they knew I would face in the corporate world. They worked us very hard, but also made sure that we were confident. They didn't just teach us complex concepts, they also instilled us with passion and inspired us. In some ways, they almost interacted with us like extended family."

To Mrs. Bethune's point, one of the first places to begin creating greater leverage and entry into the STEM-related technology world of today is through the historically black

colleges and universities servicing or communities. While

there is a tradeoff in the public recognition of HBCUs as

centers of educational excellence by the mainstream public,

these institutions provide a way of creating a large critical

mass of blacks in STEM that can spread throughout the

technology and business worlds within a short period of time.

As an example, when slavery ended, during the

Reconstruction period, African Americans in South Carolina

were allowed to attend the University of South Carolina totally

unrestricted. But this time of black advancement ended

suddenly when the state legislature passed a series of laws

separating the races, closing the doors of the college to black

students until almost one hundred years later when three

black students were allowed to attend the college in 1962.

The black community, which had a taste of the societal

possibilities that could be within their reach from attending a

school like USC, refused to let the doors of their future be

closed. In 1870, blacks founded and built two historical black colleges, like Bethune-Cookman in Florida, and in South Carolina; Benedict College and Allen University. South Carolina is also home to two other HBCUs, SC State University and Claflin University.

These four colleges have a history of producing a number of successful African Americans with degrees in a variety of fields. These individuals spread themselves throughout all portions of society. Their leadership and influence is everywhere. Their existence carries the hopes for many young black youth even today. Across the country, our HBCUs have an important place in the black history. They are a resource for erasing the STEM gap.

Black America has not leveraged the unrealized potential of its powerful postsecondary education resource to help the entire body attain the full magnitude of participation in America's technology and innovation prowess. HBCUs are still one of the critical backbones of African-American educational and economic advancement in the US. Of the approximately 7,000 higher education institutions in the

US[xxviii], there are 100 HBCUs in operation across the country[xxix] and in the US territory of the Virgin Islands. Though they make up less than 2% of the US post-secondary institutions, HBCUs educate 9.7% of the total population of African Americans enrolled in colleges and universities in the US and produce 20% of the country's African American college graduates. HBCUs also graduate 27% of the total African Americans trained in STEM[xxx]. According to the National Center for Education Statistics 2011 data, HBCU's produce an average of 10.7% of total STEM African-American graduates within all higher education institutions.

In a demonstration of equal opportunity not only of the races but also of the sexes, HBCUs have student populations that are almost 50/50 male and female. Many, like Benedict College in Columbia, SC, also produce significant numbers of post-doctoral graduates in the STEM fields. They are an important source of African American STEM talent in advanced technology industries such as alternative energy, information technology, cyber security, advanced manufacturing, biotechnology, and healthcare. HBCU researchers produce patents. Patents are the primary source of ideas for technology companies. Mining HBCU patents for use could be a source of increased black STEM participation in the technology world. In addition to targeting HBCUs for hiring, corporations should not overlook the creative innovations that might be found at HBCUs and MSIs (Minority Serving Institutions). These institutions are an un-optimized resource.

Many HBCUs were started as "land-grant" institutions in response to the Morrill Act of 1862 and the second Morrill Act of 1890. The Morrill Act's goal was to form a system of higher educational institutions in the agricultural portions of the nation during the years leading up to the Civil War and into the Reconstruction Period. Championed in Congress by Vermont Congressman Justin Smith Morrill, the original idea of a formal system of postsecondary education began in Illinois and the state of Michigan was the location of its pilot. The institutions were designed to provide instruction in the industrial and mechanical arts so that individuals living in the rural parts of the country could pursue professions of a higher level of income and with greater economic opportunity. Originally, a higher education system created for poor rural whites, the application of the educational approach expanded to include the children of free and newly emancipated blacks.

The land grant institution system developed at the state level. Each state within the US received an allocation for a number of federal acres from which it could derive initial financial funding for its initial land grant school or schools. The schools were required to have specific areas of study once organized. Engineering, agriculture science, and military training sections were three of the required study areas. The original 1862 Act enabling the funding of the land grant institutions applied to only those states that were still a part of the United States at the start of the Civil War.

After the Civil War, a second Congressional Act (i.e. the Morrill Act of 1890) extended the application of the land-grant legislation to the states that seceded during the war. In this second instance, former secession states could only establish one land grant institution for the entire state that was open to all races. If the institution was not made equally available to all of the state's residents, regardless of racial ethnicity, then another land grant institution had to be established for the races barred from attending the originally designated state land grant institution. Many southern land grant institutions refused to admit African Americans. As a result, the establishment of many secondary land grant institutions occurred for black students. The formation of many HBCUs, many of which were the secondary land grant institutions, took place during the Reconstruction period.

A map of the US showing the geographical locations of the early HBCUs would highlight that a majority of them are located in the southeastern, northeastern, and mid-Atlantic states. Additional HBCUs, founded at the beginning of the 20th century, were located in the Midwest in direct correlation to black migration patterns. Black migration to this region of the country occurred due to the growing manufacturing job opportunities as discussed earlier. This movement of the black population created large communities and a need for higher nearby education institutions. Faced with a similar discriminatory experience as schools in the South, the Midwestern schools formed because blacks were barred from land grant institutions previously established for the states' white majorities. Again, these land grant schools were developed to, and already teach, industrial and mechanical arts.

Besides the HBCUs, MSIs are a second category of educational institutions that target their services towards the black collegiate market. This classification of colleges includes the previously mentioned HBCUs along with additional institutions that also focus their support toward other ethnic minority groups such as Hispanics and Native Americans. MSIs must meet the federal government requirements of Title IV of Higher Education Act of 1965, which provides requirements for participation in the federal financial aid program funding.

MSIs, unlike the land grant institutions, are unconstrained by the maximum number allowed within a given US state and have a variety of geographical settings. There are both rural and urban settings for the colleges depending upon where their founders chose for their physical locations. A higher education institution's designation as a MSI is limited. Only those institutions where Black undergraduate enrollment is at least 25% while all other minority groups combined remain below 25% of the total student population are included in the category. The US Department of Education recognizes 470 minority-serving institutions in the US and the territories of Puerto Rico and the Virgin Islands. With over 100 HBCUs and almost 500 MSIs in place, the MSIs are significant for the black academic instruction and training. Institutions, like the University of Arkansas in Pine Bluff and Los Angeles Trade Technical College in Los Angeles, California, are MSIs helping to educate the country's African American youth in undergraduate, graduate, and post-graduate studies.

Some MSIs, unlike HBCUs, are vocational schools in the tradition of Tuskegee University founded by Booker T. Washington. One such institution, in an urban setting, is the Focus: HOPE Machinist Training Institute in Detroit, Michigan. The school is housed on a 40-acre campus in the heart of the city. It welcomes many blacks working in the automotive industry. Focus: HOPE was started by Eleanor Josaitis, a wonderful woman who I met before her death, and a Catholic priest, Father William Cunningham, as a result of the 1967 Detroit race riot. Created with a vision to "provide the city with the brightest minds that others seek not to discover", Focus: HOPE instructs and trains inner city minority youth in the skills typically found in most automotive manufacturing facilities.

The institute has trained over 2,500 students from the inner city of Detroit since its inception. In partnership with several Michigan colleges, it offers information management systems engineering, associate and bachelor engineering degree programs, as well as GED preparation courses. These programs are offered in addition to the advanced technology machinist training program for which Focus: HOPE is nationally recognized.

Together, HBCUs and MSIs already deliver a significant amount of talent to the American professional and vocational landscape. In the areas of STEM education, they provide well-trained graduates in many technology areas. With more funding and strategic planning, their capacity could easily be increased to produce more African American STEM-trained graduates. These graduates could be the primary sources of STEM talent for technology companies seeking African American workers. The schools could become the hubs for black technology startups. Google, the search technology company, recognizes this possibility. It has conducted a number of summits with HBCUs. Additionally, Google has partnered on an HBCU student scholarship, deploying its employees to help train, mentor, and recruit HBCU STEM students[xxxi].

Many HBCUs and MSIs are sitting upon scientific discoveries and patents that are awaiting industrial use in corporations and entrepreneurial ventures. Many of the colleges and universities, like most academic entities around the world, have administrative operations helping to make available the scientific discoveries made by the faculty through what are often called Technology Transfer Offices. These offices operate as the central point for organizing and communicating an individual institution's latest significant discovery. The existence of these offices at HBCUs and MSIs is a source for African American entrepreneurial opportunities in the STEM fields. As such, there undeservedly appears to be a deficiency in the black community's ability to successfully compete in developing viable companies of substantial technological importance. Herein lies another area that needs change.

During my time at GM, we regularly visited PWIs, and conferences where PWI technology transfer offices might display patents and discoveries invented by their students and faculty. We paid for inventions that would make our own products more profitable. I don't recollect us visiting HBCUs or

MSIs. It wasn't due to intentional exclusion; we just didn't know their inventions existed.

HBCU and MSI patents and discoveries need to be publicized, protected and used to help fund their institutions and launch black STEM startups. These critical resources that are owned by black Americans can counter the common misconception that black America's resources in STEM are limited. They can help efforts to build STEM prowess, provide a wellspring of young African Americans ready for employment in technology companies, and build an army of black technology entrepreneurs.

Strengthening and leveraging the invisible academic power of HBCUs and MSIs is an important first step in making these increases happen. Unfortunately, black America is in danger of losing this untapped resource that has the potential to do so much.

Despite the strong collective performance of HBCUs and MSIs in STEM-related student training and graduation, year after year these institutions continually struggle to remain financially viable. HBCUs have been hit the hardest. Some of these schools have recently closed their hallowed doors.

Moreover, economic matters facing HBCU and MSI institutions are in the news almost daily. In Washington, DC, Howard University, known as the Harvard of HBCUs, experienced a controversial 4% staff reduction between 2014 and this year. In South Carolina, South Carolina State University suffered a $50 million budget overrun and campus-wide staff reductions. The controversy around the institution's troubles led to the removal of the President, state removal of its Board of Trustees, and a threat of the college losing accreditation. As a counteraction, the alumni and students are federally suing the state for the possible failure to properly fund the school for over 40 years. In North Carolina, its legislature proposed a state budget that included reducing funds to Elizabeth City State University thus placing the school at risk of closing. There was such a public outcry towards this proposal that the reduction stalled from moving forward and was eventually killed. Instead, the legislature increased funding to the school to help it survive. Fisk University, another HBCU and MSI located in Tennessee, sold a portion of its famous art collection in order to raise much-needed funds for its operations. Its newly-resigned president, my distant relative by marriage, successfully led the school to becoming financially sound, increasing its student enrollment, and taking steps to protect its reputation as one of the top HBCUs in the country.

These are just a few examples of the ongoing and growing struggles of the HBCUs and MSIs schools servicing African Americans. Black presidents of the HBCUs state that their institutions have seen $300 million dollars of federal aid cut from their operations over the last few years. Their financial struggles are having a domino negative effect on other black educational-related organizations partnering with them. Even non-profit organizations that have traditionally worked to support these organizations are experiencing financial difficulties as a result. The United Negro College Fund (UNCF), which has 37 member HBCU schools, has resorted to accepting millions of dollars from the Koch

brothers of Koch Industries, Inc. whom many in black America

perceive as being hostile towards Democratic political

representatives and economic policies helping black

citizens[xxxii]. This state of affairs is untenable.

Despite their challenges, HBCUs and MSIs remain a

viable option for those seeking STEM education. From a

federal research funding standpoint, a majority of the HBCU

funding is awarded for STEM-related projects in areas such

as health care, nanotechnology, cyber technology,

transportation engineering, chemistry, physics, and

agricultural sciences. College graduates trained in these fields

are in high demand and command over six-figure incomes.

Technology-related grants are being awarded to the schools.

PWIs, such as Harvard University, are becoming research

partners on a more frequent basis.

Increasing endowments to HBCUs could help make

them more viable and improve their competitiveness with

PWIs. When comparing the endowments of the top PWIs with

HBCUs, the individual HBCU endowments are much smaller in monetary size by comparison[xxxiii]. With a positive viewpoint and the right strategy, increased financial resources can fund a significant STEM training movement for young African Americans at these institutions. More endowed funding could help drive increased research and generate a higher number of technology innovations by African Americans.

Perhaps a more accurate picture that black Americans need to embrace is that its collective performance in STEM, while limited, does exist. The places in which African-Americans have the ability to excel in the new technology world are not broadly visible and leveraged. Indeed, an example of a HBCU that has increased both their research and endowments to become STEM competitors to PWIs is my father's alma mater, Hampton University in Virginia. The general public remains largely unaware of the college's highly competitive capabilities. I am sure that there are other institutions suffering the same level of anonymity. With this counterintuitive view of their capabilities, blacks have a chance to turn the current picture around.

"We must shift the narrative around HBCUs from one centered on management and operational challenges to a narrative centered on the collective commitment to creative investment and innovation."[xxxiv] said Arne Duncan, the former Secretary of the US Department of Education as told to an audience of HBCU and MSI presidents at the National HBCU Week Conference in September 2013. He is right. "We want HBCUs to be known not just for their illustrious legacy of inventors like George Washington Carver but for their ongoing contributions in the world of science, technology, engineering, and math." Secretary Duncan has stated. "And we want HBCUs to be known not just for their close ties to the community, but for innovatively adapting the lessons of meaningful collaboration and partnerships with K-12, community colleges, business, philanthropy, and international exchange programs." This is the most promising path to birthing an army of blacks in STEM.

It is also proper to note here that America is home to many returning citizens who might make excellent STEM training candidates. There are many veterans who have had technical training while in the military. While they may have struggled in traditional high schools, they may have achieved mastery in military courses, like basic electricity and electronics. Like the black soldiers of World War I, some may have technical knowledge which exceeds the general public, for example, through their exposure to new innovations like drone and cybersecurity technologies. These worthy veterans should be steered toward programs where they can build on what they've accomplished. Those in the tech industry would be wise to take note of military candidates, maybe even creating on-the-job training programs specifically targeting African American veterans. This is yet another way to help build black STEM.

Finally, experts point to the endemic incarceration of black men, taking away their ability to pursue any careers at all, let alone STEM careers, as another huge loss of black

STEM capabilities. This belief has led to a massive effort on the part of political leaders of all races and political affiliations, like Democratic Senator Cory Booker of New Jersey and Republican Senator Rand Paul of Kentucky, to lead efforts within Congress to change incarceration laws. Changing the incarceration laws alone won't address the economic impact on black Americans, but it is a start. Potential STEM achievers may also be found among those previously incarcerated and creative programs could train these individuals. Governmental legal experiments like the Second Chance Pell Pilot Program, which covers a prisoner's college course and book fees, could provide a way into STEM for incarcerated black men and women[xxxv].

Finding employment is almost impossible for ex-offenders. There is no reason some could not be directed toward STEM if they have an interest once exposed to technology. STEM jobs that pay well could decrease recidivism. No doubt, some individuals will be suited for knowledge or technology-based occupations. STEM training opportunities should be encouraged.

STEM training may also be a viable option for displaced African American homemakers and mothers. Currently, many black homemakers re-enter the STEM field as Certified Nursing Assistants (CNAs) or in positions unrelated to STEM. These are minimum wage jobs. If instead, black women were redirected to full nursing programs or other STEM training like computer programming and given child care resources, many of these women could obtain STEM jobs paying well enough to support a family. This strategic approach to re-engage them in the workforce is a better option than letting them drift into fast food service or nursing assistant jobs.

In summary, a plethora of actions can help birth a black STEM army. Some actions are quick fixes and can be put in place immediately. Some actions require investigation and longer timeframes to implement. Some actions require improving the efforts already underway to help blacks in

138

STEM. Some actions require putting new efforts in places overlooked or not considered. Some actions are required of black STEMmers, themselves. There is more than enough work to go around on this issue. It will take a united front of all people interested in growing black STEM, much as it did with the Civil Rights movement.

Now that you know what more can be done, will you help?

# Chapter 5:
# Black America's Hidden Power

*"We live in a world which respects power above all things. Power, intelligently directed, can lead to more freedom."*

~ Mary McLeod Bethune, Educator and Founder of Bethune –Cookman College

*"The black fist is a meaningless symbol. When you open it, you have nothing but fingers – weak empty fingers. The only time the black fist has significance is when there's money inside. There's where the power lies."*

~ Jesse Owens, 4-time Olympic Medalist

"You have all the resources that you need to become the great thing that God wants you to be," my pastor, the honorable Reverend Dr. Charles E. Jackson, Sr., would regularly entreat our church congregation every Sunday morning. My church, at the time, was one of the largest African American churches within the entire state of South Carolina. Its name is Brookland Baptist Church of West Columbia, a suburb adjacent to the state's capital city. The church's mission was not only to bring the Christian faith to individuals and families seeking spiritual support, but also to encourage its congregants to pursue and excel in educational and economic pursuits. Almost every Sunday, Rev. Jackson would repeat this message. His delivery of these words to lift up his congregation were powerful. Listening to him caused me to think.

Both of the state's black and white populace esteemed my former church and its pastoral leadership. Brookland regularly received large monetary donations for its educational and economic endeavors from large multi-national corporations. Businesses rested assured that their donations would result in implementation of African-American empowerment programs in the local community because of the church's record of success.

Spiritual, educational, and economic development of the African peoples are the three cornerstones upon which the church engages with its followers; a very similar theology found in more black churches.

As part of my pastor's regular Sunday messages, he often reminded the congregation of an interesting fact about black financial wealth. "For every dollar that enters the African American community, it exchanges hands only three times before it exits the community and goes into the pockets of other ethnic groups. We are funding our own demise", he would exhort. "We've got to do better than this and keep the money in our own communities to build our own wealth, not the wealth of others!" These statements preceded the introduction of a business owner or entrepreneur from the church's congregation providing a brief synopsis of them and their company's goods and services. Implicit through this method of introduction was the hope that these businesses gain more patrons from the congregation thus strengthening a cycle of black wealth retention within this portion of South Carolina.

The fact is that currently, a dollar circulates within Asian communities for a month. Within Jewish communities, the timeframe is twenty days. For the Hispanics, it stays for seven days and for whites it circulates for seventeen days[xxxvi].

However, for African Americans it lasts in the community only

six hours; less than an eight-hour workday. Without knowing

it, my pastor was being generous in his comments when he

spoke to me and my fellow congregants. This is a worse

position than what I imagined. This piece of data should make

us all think.

Whenever my pastor would bring up this subject, a

picture would always come to mind. I would always envision

where there is one of numerous little creeks flowing outward

from the black community to other communities with no

returning water. Because no water is returning, the creeks are

diminishing and in danger of running dry; an analogy of the

situation faced by African-Americans and reflective of the

picture crafted by the media. It was a frightening picture to

me. So I spent time investigating the details. I learned that the

picture inside my head, and probably inside the heads of

many others, is too negatively skewed with regard to the

financial status of black America and its current wealth

position. Blacks command more financial power than many realize. Recognition of this fact can help generate black STEM wealth.

Before we go into a discussion of the financial strategy to create black STEM wealth, let's first consider if blacks need financial support for their own technology and innovations.

One of the ideas, when thinking about ways of increasing black STEM efforts in the country, is that it only pertains to K-12 education, collegiate pursuits, and corporate employment. This is not true. Increasing African American STEM presence is also needed in technology-related entrepreneurial efforts. Blacks have a history of producing innovation in the US as was discussed in an earlier chapter. They continue to produce innovations today. These innovations are rarely funded outside of the academic world. African Americans need to retain their money longer so it can help fund the million and billion dollar business ideas that aren't seeing the light of day.

There are many black inventors, scientists and tech entrepreneurs creating new innovations across the country. Examples of these people are

**Christopher Gray** - a serial entrepreneur, investor, and winner of over 1.3 million dollars in scholarships. He leads the team that developed *Scholly*, a 99 cent app that helps student search for scholarships. His successful pitch on NBC's Shark Tank lead to an emotional explosion on the set.

**Will.i.am** – the Grammy Award-winning singer, songwriter, and Intel's Director of Creative Innovation, is known for embracing all things high tech and has recent intentions to invest in Israeli tech companies. He has also been involved with the US's annual FIRST Robotics Competition, NASA initiatives, and entrepreneurial efforts associated with Apple Corporation's iPhone and his own super-luxury high tech automotive effort, called IAMAUTO. His i.am.angel Foundation raises money to provide scholarships to kids in STEAM (i.e. STEM with A for the arts).

**Dr. Dre** - a hip hop master, and one of the newest black billionaires, with his recent sell of Beats Electronics to Apple. He demonstrated the successful high growth of a multi-billion dollar entrepreneurial effort using new technology to make a niche in the saturated music headphone market.

**Jewel Burks** – Co-founder and Chief Executive Officer of PartPic, Inc, a million dollar-funded startup company that uses proprietary visual recognition software technology to identify products for purchase by online customers.

There are blacks who have been and are inventing, tinkering, and working on inventions in their homes, garages, and basements. There are blacks, men and women, who have been writing code for years. "In the 70s, I remember writing code while my supervisor stood over me watching." said Gloria Anderson Riddick, who is also a gospel singer, sharing some of her earlier career experiences. "He couldn't believe a black woman could write code."

American society needs to acknowledge these innovators and their efforts.

As black America struggles with its ability to generate STEM talent through the educational system pipeline, which includes HBCU increases, it needs a targeted strategy for financing STEM initiatives. Two tactics available to achieve this goal are:

- Refocus money donated to colleges producing STEM talent; and

- Create partnerships with black financial institutions (including investment entities) for black technology funding expansion.

HBCUs that service blacks in technology training and develop most of the technology innovations in the community are struggling with their daily operations as individual institutions. Some have used their endowment funds to bridge financing gaps for their operations. A key to building black STEM capabilities is making endowment funds work more effectively, which requires steering this type of fund away from supporting daily operations at HBCUs to STEM and STEM-related initiatives.

Most higher education institutions within the US have endowments. Endowments are created from large amounts of money that colleges and universities have received from many donors. The donors may or may not be alumni of the institution to which they made the donation as this is not a requirement. Most donors provide the money in order to establish student scholarships, professorships for the school's faculty, and the construction of new facilities in their name. Endowment money received from donors can also be used to fund athletics for the institution, new institutional programs, and medical and scientific research and innovation. Endowment funds without donor-specified restrictions are often used to support an institution's operations or a special initiative identified by the school. These "quasi-endowment" gifts are relied upon especially during periods of economic difficulties for the institution or the country such as the global recession of 2007-2009. Specified monetary uses of the funds are contractually specified by the donor at the time of their gift giving.

The Duke Endowment, for example, is a well-known, much respected, and highly regarded fund within the Carolinas. The Duke Endowment was established by James Duke, the patriarch of the tobacco products Duke family of Durham, North Carolina, my hometown. The fund, which was $3.4 billion in size as of 2014, provides grants and funding for health care, higher education, child care, and rural church funding. To receive funding from this endowment is an honor and a symbol of prestige for the awardees. As such, many organizations desiring funds to support work out of Duke's primary areas still make appeals to the organization. However, the Duke Endowment funding priorities do not change and they work with their awardees to ensure there is no unapproved mission growth causing these funds to be used for other activities. This type of laser-focused approach in endowment STEM mission needs enactment at HBCUs if they are to thrive.

Universities and colleges are motivated to increase the size of their endowments on a continual basis. Large institutions, like Harvard and Yale, accumulate large financial reserves (over $30 and $19 billion respectively) in their endowments and manage their operations such that the money is not used to acquire physical assets or encumbered by debt to pay staff or construct new facilities. Institutions with smaller endowments, on the other hand, struggle with this approach as their funds are often used to finance every day operations and the future employment of the fund's administrative staff. HBCUs fall into this latter category. The goal of a majority of endowments is to contain enough monetary value so that the fund's return on investment covers the investment cost of managing the fund, yearly increases in expenses due to inflation, and money spent by the institution for its operational needs.  Getting this right is a delicate balance.

In order for the black community to expand its impact and grow its prosperity through STEM, a more targeted donor approach with endowments must be pursued. More donors, both within and outside of black communities, should be identified to help build upon the financial resources already in place. Not only should African American college alumni strive to increase their fund donations to institutions that specifically service a majority of our community, but these increased dollars should also be required to fund STEM-related research and initiatives within a market-matching short timetable. For technology-related initiatives, this means that the endowments are not to continue on until perpetuity, but are to be expended within a 5 to 10 year timeframe.

Changes also need to be made to endowment boards and oversight committees memberships. Rather than generically appoint or elect individuals with strong business backgrounds to these groups, individuals with success in developing and marketing technologies or leading STEM-related initiatives should be targeted for membership. With the experience and knowledge of these individuals, African American institutions can make informed decisions to route their endowment funds to well-planned initiatives in areas like medical research where advances in cancer, diabetes, obesity, and mental health diseases can be accelerated to benefit the health of blacks while at the same time generate millions of dollars. Additionally, initiatives in the scientific fields of chemistry, physics, genomics, and engineering that primarily benefit the black community could also be funded with thoughtful leadership. These changes are minor adjustments to the way in which the black people handle the financial blessing that it has with its HBCU endowments, but these changes could help to make a world of difference.

This is one avenue to achieve increased STEM work through donor funding. There are other avenues for retaining black wealth. STEM-related program partnerships with black-owned financial institutions can help, also.

# Chapter 6:
# Black Money Fists

*"God helps those who help themselves."*

~ Benjamin Franklin, US Founding Father, Inventor and Scientist

While living in South Carolina, I learned about the historic activities within the African-American community to counter the effects of economic deprivation upon its population. African-Americans suffered from a lack of access to mainstream capital to start their own businesses and organizations. The solution used by the blacks at the turn of the 20th century, which has been used effectively by other ethnic groups since, was to combine its money to build its own engine of prosperity. These "mutual aid societies" proved quite effective in helping blacks achieve economically. One story in which a revered South Carolinian used this strategy involves Ms. Modjeska Simkins and the defunct Victory Savings Bank.

Born December 5, 1899 in Columbia, SC, she is considered one of the mothers of the South Carolina civil rights movement[xxxvii]. Named by her mother after a well-known Polish actress of the late 1800s, Madame Helena Mojeska, Ms. Simkins became a major force for African American equality. A graduate of Benedict College, Ms. Simkins was a teacher at the city's Booker T. Washington High School at the start of her career. She was instrumental in writing the lawsuit declaration for one of the South Carolina schools participating in the *Brown v. Board of Education, Topeka KS* US Supreme Court case. One of Modjeska's legacies was the early work that she did to help establish a bank for black workers that needed money when denied access to capital due to their anti-segregation and political activities. The Victory Savings Bank was organized by I.J. Joseph, I.S. Leevy, and C.E. Stephenson of Columbia and chartered in 1921[xxxviii]. These individuals, along with Ms. Simkins and others, used the financial construct to help black America lift itself up when the financial resources were needed the most.

The black-owned banking system remains a significant power that is not widely acknowledged and recognized by many people, both inside and outside of black circles. The banks have provided access to desperately needed financial resources when other options were nonexistent or severely limited. The first black-owned bank was chartered on March 3, 1888 and would open its door for business one year later. Its name was the Savings Bank of the Grand Fountain United Order of the True Reformers or, for short, The True Reformers Savings Bank and it was located in Virginia[xxxix]. The bank was an extension of the most powerful fraternal and business organizations in the nation for African Americans at the time called the United Order of the True Reformers. At the peak of its activity, it had more than $1 million (USD) in deposits. The bank's president was William Washington Brown who believed, as Booker T. Washington did, that the black community's success should not be dependent upon the white public of the time. "Let us stop playing, trifling, and wasting our time and talents, and scattering our little mites to the four winds of the earth, and let us unite ourselves in a solid band."

155

This message is similar to the one delivered by my pastor encouraging the retention of black money today. The True Reformers Savings Bank was a model for several other black-owned banks that would follow such as the Mechanics Savings Bank, the famous Richmond, Virginia St. Luke Penny Savings Bank, founded by Ms. Margaret (Maggie) Lena Walker (the first African American woman president of an American bank), the Second Street Savings Bank (also of Richmond, Virginia) and Ms. Simkin's Victory Savings Bank.

Today, there are nineteen leading Black founded banks within the US and a handful of smaller black-owned community banks in the US. Many of the leading African American banks, unlike the J.P. Morgan and Goldman Sachs of the country, are located in highly urban communities. They control significant capital that can be used to help advance a major STEM technology initiative. A partnership needs to be formed between these black banks and groups seeking to help fund black technology entrepreneurs.

This is hidden power that if leveraged in conjunction with the educational juggernaut of the HBCUs and MSIs could result in significant gains in the STEM fields.

# Chapter 7:
# A Collective STEM Ambition

*"We cannot seek
achievement for ourselves
and forget about progress
and prosperity for our
community...Our
ambitions must be broad
enough to include the
aspirations and needs of
others, for their sakes and
for our own."*

~ Cesar Chavez, Labor Leader and
Civil Rights Activist

It is easy to look at today's black community, watch its
struggles and exclusion from the knowledge-based society,
and take no action to help. It is important to realize that this
has a cascading effect and will eventually impact the
economic fortunes of the US. Leaders of all races who
understand the disastrous outcome of this problem are
already engaged in finding solutions. More leaders are joining
the fight almost daily.  It will take all Americans to address the
persistent systemic and racial issues of this century like it did

with the Civil Rights movement of the previous one. Everyone must get involved.

One of the great lessons coming out of the Great Recession of 2009 is a concept called "collective ambition", first articulated by Harvard researchers[xl]. The central idea behind the concept is that with the right construction of integrated and collaborative approaches, a group of leaders and their employees (or, in this case, constituents) can successfully survive and thrive during difficult economic periods. Built upon the results gleaned from the analysis of nationally administered surveys, the Harvard researchers developed the model consisting of two aspects (i.e. "glue" and "grease") and seven key elements. The "glue" is engagement through continual collaborations and the "grease" is disciplined execution of the engagement. The seven elements are:

1. A central overriding purpose or reason for existing;

2. A vision of things to be achieved within a specified period of time;

3. A list of targets and milestones that will be used to measure progress towards the vision;

4. A prioritized list of strategic and operational actions to be taken to pursue the vision;

5. A list of the commitments made to the constituents and stakeholders concerning the outcome of the effort;

6. A group of core values that are the guiding principles for which the leaders and constituents stand; and

7. A leadership behavior construct providing direction for administration of day-to-day activities.

Above all these things, however, is the need to have an authentic purpose for why the actions of the leaders and constituents are taking place. Without this subordinate focus, all subsequent actions struggle to be effective and sustainable enough for things to positively progress through painful times.

For African-Americans who participate in the traditional religious experiences of the community, the Harvard model of collective ambition occur every week. Most longstanding black churches in the US are examples of the collective ambition model in action. Many black churches suffer from difficult financial circumstances threatening their ongoing viability on a regular basis. Nevertheless, many of these same churches continue year after year to survive and grow. Pastors annually cast out their vision of the church for the ensuing year. Congregants are brought together for a service commonly referred to as "vision casting" so that they can hear the pastor's vision, and understand the strategic and operational priorities for the church staff and administration. Churches which do vision casting highlight the targets and milestones for the body and remind the congregants about the overriding promise of their faith, the purpose of the church's existence, and the core values espoused by the church body. Subsequent messages, programs, and themes emphasize the acceptable and expected behaviors of the church leaders, the various stakeholders involved with the church, and their progress in achieving the overriding church goals. Many places of worship outside of the traditional black church also use a similar model.

A second instance in which African-Americans are familiar with the concept of collective ambition is with the Civil Rights Movement of the 1950s and 60s. The leaders of the Civil Rights movement had a vision of the full realization of the US Constitution on their behalf. The promise for them was liberty and justice for all. They strategically focused on changes in the interstate commerce treatment of African-Americans by attacking the ill treatment in diners, restaurants, and on public transportation, namely buses. They then attached the separate, but equal treatment concerning the US educational system. Successes in getting changes in these two areas led to African Americans receiving federal protections for the right to vote. Achieving these three objectives required a great deal of collaboration and decisive action with all Americans on the part of the leaders. This was accomplished despite the naysayers, quarterback pundits, and those watching from the sidelines. Although the process received its formal name fifty years later, the collective ambition model was its framework.

The leadership behavior adopted was one of personal dignity and quiet resolve to help them with their messaging. The Civil Rights Movement's core values were nonviolence, demonstrations, and achieving meaningful adherence to legislation. The original Civil Rights movement leaders painted a picture of economic opportunity and personal safety as the commitments to the stakeholders for participating in the controversial movement. Their timeframe for achieving the goals of the movement was the only element of the collective ambition model that was not clearly defined. However, they were able to achieve all of their goals within 14 years (i.e. 1954 – 68) from the start of their effort. It was a shared commitment that encouraged Americans of all races to join in to help.

Considering this model, it is conceivable that a new civil rights movement could be started to increase widespread black participation in STEM and innovation. A vertically integrated model of activity that supports STEM immersion from the time an African-American is born until their career's end would be the result. The question is - What would it take to organize this effort using to the collective ambition model as a roadmap? What would the components of the effort include?

These questions are at the forefront of many academic, community, and governmental policy discussions occurring in the US as evidenced by an October 2013 conference hosted by Stanford University in cooperation with Kapor Capital, Facebook, Google, various HBCUs, and several other notable organizations within the US. Subsequent gatherings of leaders building black STEM programs have asked and are asking these same questions. They are at the beginning steps of the collective ambition process. But are they enough for a movement to swell and begin to take place?

I answer this question through the recommendation of a comprehensive framework uniquely combining approaches and methods for increased African American technological innovation. The roadmap is designed specifically for increasing the research capabilities and outcomes in places where significant sources of black STEM talent and capabilities reside. I also recommend that the goals and objectives of the framework be structured through the application of four key aims:

## A National Black STEM 2020 Initiative

1.  The establishment of a national black STEM vision and strategy that uses an inclusive collaboration framework with all institutions, businesses, and grassroots organizations to involve and integrate resources working on this issue;

2.  The implementation of a well-coordinated funding model involving black-owned financial institutions, high net worth African Americans, and traditional and non-traditional funding mechanisms to leverage financial resources that are underutilized;

3.  The creation of a national talent tracking tool to ensure that STEM-trained African American college

graduates, academic researchers, corporate

employees, and technology entrepreneurs are

connected with one another, monitored, and provided

mentorship support to continue their advancement;

and

4. The creation of a performance tracking and evaluation

   system to measure and communicate the national

   initiative's progress to desired outcomes.

The initiative should have a goal for a 100% increase in

current African American STEM output through the ecosystem

over the next 3 to 5 years.

This synergistic approach is similar to the collective

ambition model upon which the first civil rights movement

organically grew by itself and the Harvard model. This familiar

hybrid model has a high chance of succeeding if applied.

The remaining sections of this chapter walk through

details of this national strategy proposal. The information can

be a little weighty for those who are not leading black STEM initiatives. I suggest you read read this information in bite-sized intervals. Don't get caught up in the details. Understanding the overall concept is what counts.

If you're a leader working on the black STEM problem, I recommend reading the rest of the chapter and discussing the content with fellow leaders as part of a diversity and inclusion workshop. Hearing ideas generated from these sections should make for a lively discussion. I hope that at the end of your debate, meaningful and more beneficial actions can start.

Let's begin our wade a little deeper into the black STEM water.


**Creating a Smarter Village**

To attack the issue of too few African Americans in the STEM fields, an integrated strategy using five approaches will have the greatest impact in changing the current condition and can be accomplished within a short period of time. The strategy must be integrated so that the problem can be addressed in a holistic manner because of the systemic nature of the problem. The five approaches recommended are:

- Increasing the research pipeline volume of "meaningful" (i.e. research that can be used by industry) STEM activity and measure the community's performance against a set of actionable metrics;

- Improving the coordination of efforts by all stakeholders working to address the STEM deficiency issues for blacks along the entire lifetime continuum;

- Increasing the use of data and information technology to enhance African American understanding of the highest impact actions affecting sustainable change;

- Leveraging the financial investment resources controlled and managed by African Americans towards strategic support of STEM research at HBCUs, MSIs,

and entrepreneurial efforts within relevant startup
incubators; and

- Forming partnerships within the black media to more
regularly and broadly publicize to all Americans the
current STEM accomplishments and opportunities.


These approaches are not unique nor are they
complicated, but they do require a higher level of cooperation
and coordination around the issue of STEM advancement.
Attempting to focus on one singular approach more than
others will result in marginal success due to the fact that these
approaches impact various portions of the black ecosystem
and therefore are synergistically dependent upon on another.
This is a complex, interconnected systemic issue that requires
a systemic approach. In many ways, this is the black
community's 21st century's virtual civil rights issue. And just as
the black movements of the past, it will require involvement
and cooperation of the entire body to tackle the myriad of

issues that exist. This is the reason I suggest a national strategy. Understanding the pipeline of issues and the community's current and desired performance along the entire pipeline is a key first step to building this strategy.

**Develop an End-to-End Pipeline**

One of the most immediate and visible approaches already underway is working to increase the pipeline of African Americans entering and advancing in STEM. As discussed earlier, there are numerous and varied efforts underway to introduce programs to increase the number of K-12 black students showing an interest and entering into the pipeline of STEM study. There are also several collegiate programs funded by the federal government that seek to help increase the number of black STEM researchers and their research opportunities. Programs such as HBCU-UP (i.e. HBCU Undergraduate Program) are structured so that young black STEM talent in the pipeline can be more easily identified and mentored while working to obtain the undergraduate,

graduate, and post-graduate degrees. African American

professional associations such as BPDA (the Black Processor

Data Association), the Society of Black Engineers, other

STEM-related associations of the majority, and corporations

all have programs in place to help mentor young and mid-

career professionals for successful STEM careers. Ancillary

entities such as the previously mentioned high tech incubators

are focused on the pipeline of African Americans

entrepreneurs within the STEM industries. While all of these

efforts represent a great deal of activity, they are disparate

and not integrated. The result is a great deal of work, but

minimal visible results.

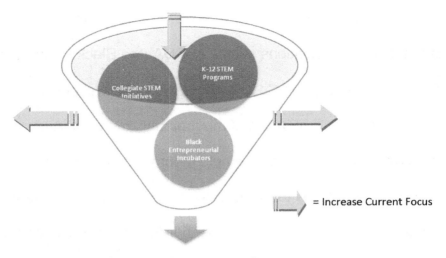

K-12 STEM Programs

Collegiate STEM Initiatives

Black Entrepreneurial Incubators

= Increase Current Focus

African American STEM Pipeline

Rather than examine the results and impact of these individual efforts along the black STEM pipeline, a more integrated and comprehensive review of the cumulative pipeline efforts is needed for greater and timelier results. From the beginning of the STEM pipeline to its end, African Americans should be measuring the cumulative result of these various pipeline initiatives to determine what is having the greatest and least amount of impact; where initiatives are generating the greatest amount of impact, more support (both financially and formally) should be provided by all members. These evidence-based initiatives should also be replicated and measured for their continued performance monitoring. Initiatives not resulting in significant impacts should be minimized and discontinued so that the resources involved can be deployed to more beneficial pipeline activities.

The cumulative Black STEM pipeline also needs be evaluated for areas where critical gaps in focus exist so that actions can be taken in these key areas as well. For example, there are many private and public efforts to address the black human capital shortage in the STEM fields as this is one of the most obvious shortfalls to advancing African Americans in STEM. However, no effort has been made to date to understand how these programs and initiatives may overlap and be redundant to one another. There has also been no work completed to determine if the programs are producing sustainable results over the long term (i.e. greater than three years) and how they are affecting other aspects of the pipeline such as the amount of downstream black STEM entrepreneurial investment, the number of African American corporate leaders in the STEM fields, and growth (or lack of growth) over time. These are important pieces of information that need to be understood to determine the adjustments that must be made to enable increases in the output of the entire pipeline.

Another example of a black STEM pipeline area needing a more holistic and comprehensive strategy is in the area of patents and trade secrets. Many of the HBCUs and MSIs have technology transfer offices in their organizations, as also mentioned earlier, yet many of these offices have difficulty broadly publicizing their researchers' patent and research discovery results to the financial, entrepreneurial, and corporate arms of the black community and the public at-large. This portion of the pipeline is, in a sense, "hidden" from the rest of the pipeline. This invisible resource may be resulting in potentially new STEM-related products and services languishing away from the global marketplace.

A full analysis of the entire black STEM pipeline is needed so that a more comprehensive plan of addressing the pipeline volume and performance can be established. This recommended approach would help to better prioritize its time and monetary support of effective pipeline initiatives resulting in new black-owned technology businesses and more high-paying jobs. Having this information would provide a better understanding of the overall long term pipeline performance across an entire STEM-trained black person's life.

The next approach that would be of benefit to a black STEM initiative is the umbrella coordination of the disparate and disjointed efforts occurring along the entire black life continuum and STEM pipeline. To accomplish this, a consortium is needed. There are currently a myriad of consortiums already active. A lean virtually orchestrated national consortium could coordinate cross-sharing of information from all the rest. Let's see next how we might accomplish this.

## Build an Ecosystem of Collaboration

Whenever a group of people are facing a major issue or initiative, the formation of a stakeholder workgroup to address the issue is the approach most advised and usually taken. The idea of a stakeholder workgroup is two-fold; bring together the people affected by an issue so that their knowledge of its various aspects can be captured and included for a more robust design of the solution. The creation of a stakeholder workgroup also helps to solidify support of the effort's outcomes so that its implementation can occur unimpeded.  When looking at the old adage "it takes a village..." to help address a young person's capabilities, the same can be said of addressing the black STEM issue. There are many stakeholder workgroups that already have formed and their memberships contain many of the brightest minds and top leaders.  The question that is outstanding is how do these stakeholder workgroups collectively know that they are doing well with the resources at their disposal given their current disparate and uncombined approach to coordination?

Is there a way that their individual resources could be better coordinated and leveraged to produce greater results as compared to the results achieved currently? Is there a "smarter" way for the village?

Stakeholder workgroups work well and generate results when they are meaningfully inclusive of all stakeholder groups, well planned, results-focused, and transparent. Stakeholder workgroups, however, can also be self-defeating if their missions become too broad, unfocused and their participants become too numerous for effective coordination. The black community is suffering from too many uncoordinated stakeholder workgroups that do not have all of the relevant parties seated at the table. This lack of centralized holistic collaboration and cooperation across the ecosystem is resulting in suboptimal results as it pertains to the amount of money and man-hours being applied to address the black STEM technology development shortfall.

When looking at the HBCUs and MSIs, as an example, there are several different consortiums and stakeholder groups that are actively involved in addressing Black STEM issues. The groups typically involve the administrative leaders of the organizations who meet on a regular basis. These are powerful groups filled with individuals who are key decision-makers in determining the future of black STEM.

However, upon closer examination of these stakeholder groups, an unsettling fact begins to emerge. Many of these stakeholder groups have overlapping missions, goals, and objectives. The groups also have many of the same leaders representing a small portion of the stakeholders in the entire black STEM ecosystem. The stakeholders primarily represented are from academia or from government with no connection to the entrepreneurial and investment arms of black innovation. Conferences held with the non-academic stakeholders of the Black STEM universe do not often result in formalized plans that are publicly tracked and evaluated for their performance over time. It is questionable whether or not these groups are achieving an acceptable return on investment (or ROI) of their participants' time given the redundancy which appears to exist among them.

The recommendation presented here is that an umbrella consortium, consisting of representatives of the entire BLACK STEM ecosystem, be created and that one comprehensive mission with measurable goals and objectives be established. This would be similar to the work done in the Civil Rights movement under the leadership of Dr. Martin Luther King, Jr. This consortium will be different in that it is led first and foremost by transparent collaboration and performance metrics. It will also focus on moving as quickly and being as agile as possible. The goal of the consortium will be three-fold:

1. Increasing the quantifiable "value" of the black STEM output in the local, regional, and global marketplaces;

2. Increasing the tangible competitiveness of the Black STEM individuals and organizations within the ecosystem; and

3. Identifying and using non-traditional approaches to significantly increasing financial resources to significantly grow the Black STEM capabilities.

The consortium will operate with all members committed to using the concept of "co-opetition" to meet its goals and objectives. Co-opetition is the process or methodology of cooperating towards a common goal while maintaining individual competitive positioning and activities. The approach protects the areas of competition and finds the areas of cooperation. The aims of the co-opetition is threefold; to increase the African American community's competitiveness in STEM, to increase funding in support of specific black STEM outcomes, and to increase the value and return on investment of the national effort.

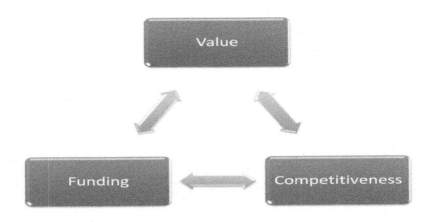

**Figure 1:** Balanced STEM Consortium Aims

In other words, with an umbrella consortium implementing a national strategy, Black STEM leadership coordination across the country would move from this:

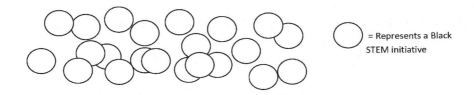

= Represents a Black STEM initiative

to this:

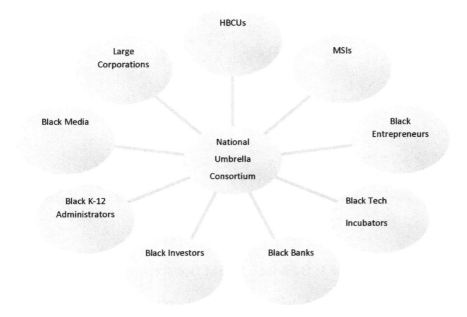

A recent example where this type of approach has been used to facilitate a significant change in an aspect of American life is the consortiums that were established and involved with setting new policies for the changes to the health care industry as outlined in the Patient Protection and Affordable Care Act. The US health care system had become too costly and too exclusionary to effectively service a large portion of the American public. Health care system outcomes had also become ineffective in producing healthy individuals to compete in the global marketplace. Consortiums, with representatives from the entire US health care ecosystem, were chartered by the federal government to develop a comprehensive and holistic new vision for the nation's health care system. Stakeholders involved committed themselves to making sure the healthcare ecosystem changes were a success. Despite many issues along the way, the national consortium approach worked. Implementation of the law changed the ways in which Americans interacted with their health care providers and insurers within four years. It is doubtful a non-umbrella consortium approach would achieve the same results in such a short time.

It is different from other past efforts in that it is guided first and foremost by highly transparent collaboration and performance metrics that span the entire spectrum of the African American technology ecosystem. The consortium or strategic leadership workgroup is also focused on moving quickly and being as agile as possible. This urgent pace for action will not allow for a top-heavy bureaucratic format. The consortium's sole purpose will be providing a leadership team through which overall project strategies can be developed, governing policies of the resulting collaborations established, and removal of roadblocks to the overall success.

The consortium framework minimizes the financial burden of individual HBCU and MSI efforts. Similar consortiums exist with the larger universities and research groups within the US. A similar organization in South Carolina was able to increase its multi-million dollar funding capabilities by 100% as a result of forming a health research consortium. I used to work for the organization, called Health Sciences South Carolina. Although the organization's members struggled initially with the concept, they were operating like a well-oiled machine by the time I left their employment. Once again, the biggest measure of success was that the consortium produced significant value to the South Carolina health care ecosystem.

The goals of the black STEM consortium will be to organize the ecosystem for more effectiveness, analyze opportunities and challenges, and act with decisiveness using a laser-focused speed. Governance will include adopting Memorandums of Understanding (MOUs) and Data Use and Reciprocal Support Agreements (DURSAs), like those used in the health care industry, which explicitly detail the use allowable for shared data within the consortium. Additionally, the group will determine the privacy and security standards by which the organizations use and share their combined information. This will ensure that sensitive information does not fall into the hand of groups with malicious intent trying to derail the effort.

## Collect and Analyze Data

One of my major discoveries during the research of this document was the tremendous amount of data that exists on the black community and its relationship (or lack thereof) to the STEM and innovation wave hitting the country. Research has been done to understand almost every facet of African American life in the US and more information is continually being released about black America's lagging position and opportunities within the new global technology society. Unfortunately, very little of this information has been brought together before now to create a complete and analytical assessment of the factors affecting the limited black STEM participation and possible comprehensive solutions to the current problem. A comprehensive and centralized repository is needed for this data to formulate an intelligent national strategy for a comprehensive black STEM plan.

In the innovation society, data is the "new oil" and data analytics is the "new engine" upon which decisions about addressing complex subjects can be made. Companies, governments, and organizations (both large and small) are all gathering data about the issues that are of most interest and learning how to analyze that data for the greatest market impact. Black Americans need to undertake a data initiative to understand more completely what must be done to increase its STEM activities. Looking at certain aspects is a good start, but understanding the universe of issues affecting black's relationship to STEM needs to be better and more quickly researched if a significant change is to occur. A logical place for the work to begin is with the black-servicing educational institutions within the country; the HBCUs and MSIs.

As in other industries, the education field is beginning to embrace large bodies of data (i.e. Big Data) and data analytics to assess the effectiveness of it systems and proactively forecast its future needs. This requires leveraging the use of information technology tools and methods to accomplish this task. In a recent December 2013 Request for Information (RFI) by the US Department of Defense, the federal agency sought to gather data about the STEM research capabilities of HBCUs and MSIs. Other individual HBCU/MSI data collection efforts, such as the online data website "HBCU-Levers" by the Digital Learning Lab, provide examples of the ways in which increased statistical data analysis can help provide improved strategic and operational guidance for the institutions. Additionally, the federal government is rewarding greater black researcher collaboration through financial incentives. Benefiting from each of these requires implementing a master network augmented by data analytics to identify effective black STEM results. Data mapping, a common ontology, an inclusive and transparent data exchange, and predictive modeling enable quantification of the best consortium and HBCUs opportunities. I know this sounds confusing, but it works.

External to the black education portion of the ecosystem, financial data about black technology entrepreneurship needs collection and analysis. There is a great deal of untapped opportunity within the social media-related platforms of non-traditional crowdfunding areas which could benefit blacks. More data needs to be shared about black endowment levels. More financial assessments about the black management of its overall financial resource and STEM are needed. The impact of this will be to deploy higher ROI activities throughout the ecosystem.

Is this making sense? Or do you feel overwhelmed? More simplistically, the objectives in the data area for the umbrella consortium will be:

- Collect and refine the relevant data;

- Filter and assess the accuracy of the data; and

- Use analytics to improve decision making as to the actions needed.

In some regard, it can be said that in order for the black community to increase its understanding of its relationship to the world of STEM and innovation, it needs to undertake innovative STEM approaches in order to succeed. What an interesting conundrum this presents.

As indicated, radical steps are needed to change black America's current relationship to the world of science, technology, and innovation. To do this the collective must have more centralized and comprehensive information about itself in this aspect. It will require a major shift in thinking. A mental paradigm shift to do this will be needed. I hope that

many of you reading this book are ready to start.

# Chapter 8:
# Surviving the Culture

*"Then join hand in hand, brave
Americans all,
By uniting we stand, by
dividing we fall;
In so righteous a cause let us
hope to succeed,
For heaven approves of each
generous deed.."*
~ John Dickinson, "Penman of the Revolution"
*The Liberty Song, 1768*

*"And if a house be divided against itself,
that house cannot stand."*
~ Mark 3:25 King James Version

If we are to survive as a nation in this information age,
then we must survive together. If we remain divided, we will
surely fail.

It is disingenuous to lay the entire blame for African
America's failure to keep pace with the STEM revolution at the
black America's feet. The history of black technology
endeavors in the US, as detailed earlier in this book, present
the case against solely blaming blacks. As the black

community works to make inroads, it cannot be left unsaid that mainstream America, white America, has a role to play. Efforts to move black STEM forward will be for nothing unless white America, especially white corporate America, is willing to embrace black America as part of the STEM team. White America must be willing to educate, support the education of, hire, establish partnerships, and contract with black Americans.

A former STEM employee shared her experience. "I worked at a Navy Hospital at the base where the Navy War College is located. The local blacks nicknamed the base 'the country club' because it was almost impossible for black people to get hired there, even veterans. The Navy War College (where the Navy's most senior officers are trained), like many of the other commands there, were virtually all white. I fought hard to get employed there. I was overqualified for the job I finally landed, a lower-level STEM-related job. Most of the people there were civil, some were very welcoming and treated me like a fellow human being. But there was a group of hostile white male bullies who harassed me and made my work life unbearable.

They didn't harass me because I wasn't qualified or didn't do my job: I got excellent performance appraisals and excellent reviews; I even got a special mention during a Navy Inspector General review. The better I performed, the more they resented me. The bullies begrudged my presence, even at the low grade level. The bullies didn't want me there; I was out of my place. They resented that I might seek promotion."

It is a fabrication when white America says there are no qualified STEM candidates just as other industries claim a lack of qualified black managers, writers, and artists. It is a convenient lie for those who want to keep things as they are. Black America knows it is a lie because the qualified, but unemployed, reside in our communities.

A young female engineer that I know is an example of a talented engineer who remains unemployed despite her credentials. This young woman has been searching for a job for almost a year. She has an undergraduate degree in mechanical engineering, a Master of Science degree in aerospace, aeronautical, and astronautical engineering, and a PhD in energy and mineral engineering. She was a Sloan Fellow and the recipient of endowed fellowship. She worked for one of the US National Laboratories and the US Department of Energy. She has three publications on power and renewable energy. She had received numerous endorsements of her work from former peers. She is a personable and likeable. Nevertheless, surprisingly, she cannot find work despite living in the Raleigh-Durham, NC area with hundreds of technology companies. She has been shut out. And yet, companies claim there are no people like her available to fill their STEM-related jobs.

I know the lack of employment for blacks trained in STEM is true because I have been unemployed for almost two years while white employers dismiss me with the modern day equivalent of "For Whites Only" signs: "You're overqualified" or "You're too inexperienced" or "You're not what we had in mind." I've managed billion dollar corporate budgets, led international departments of product engineers, designed parts in General Motors vehicles, advised state legislators on complex technology implementations, and recently started learning to code. Yet, I am not able to find employment. This is so ridiculous that the local Durham, NC unemployment office sends me notices about customer service representative and grocery clerk jobs (both also minimum wage jobs) because they have given up finding positions for me in my field. I've attended unemployment classes with black software developers, network engineers, and social media market analysts with multiple years of experience desperately looking for work. No qualified blacks available to fill corporate technology jobs? That is a lie. Don't believe it.

The current lack of employment for STEM-trained blacks is worse than when I graduated from my undergraduate program. But the unwelcoming tactics are still the same. When I graduated from college and began my first job with General Motors, I was hired as a junior engineer working in a manufacturing facility in an area that made parts for car chassis. The area was located in a part of the building hidden in a faraway corner which management rarely visited. It was a challenging job in a difficult environment. Even though I had performed well in my studies and previous internships with the company, I was placed under greater scrutiny. I was black and a female, two characteristics that some thought would result in a short career with the company because I wouldn't be able to measure up. As my later career would demonstrate, both of those assumptions were proven to be false. The implicit message was that I had to earn my way into the ranks of engineers qualified to practice the craft.

Unlike most of my classmates, I worked second shift from 12pm to 4am in the morning. Many of my white classmates with engineering degrees, upon graduation, got jobs in nice offices in other parts of the company. While it seemed strange, I did not complain; I was thankful for the job. I needed the job to prove to myself that the last five years of my life working towards entry into a white male-dominated career was not a waste of my time.

I also did not want to be one of those students without a job at the end of their college years. It was 1985, the Reagan years, and jobs were difficult to find. Even with a technical degree, companies like General Motors (with whom I interned), were hesitant to hire new college graduates due to the associated employment costs and their struggling profits in an uncertain economy. Affirmative action was just starting to come under attack after a brief period of success in opening the doors of many companies to technically educated African Americans.

The first hiring preference at General Motors was white males who had backgrounds tinkering on cars in addition to their possessing an engineering degree. Black men and white women were next in line for acceptance. Black women engineers in automotive were chosen last in most hiring decisions. Black women engineers were still a rarity. Many white male engineers in the industry viewed this new group of engineers as being "tokens" to fulfill an unfair hiring quota.

They resisted accepting us through their constant antagonistic behaviors towards us.

Antagonistic actions against engineering recruits included making new hires clean up conference rooms after meetings, assigning them to coffee pot refill duty for an entire shift (especially if a female), or assigning them to the dangerous task of crawling in and out of running conveyor belts to make sure product was moving along unhindered throughout the system (even though they knew it wasn't necessary).

In the public eye, there appeared to be many companies promoting their affirmative action efforts with marketing campaigns stressing their need to do more. It was similar to all the diversity hiring press being spread by corporations today. Behind the scenes, however, companies were filled with employees and leaders questioning the need for diversity in their technical ranks altogether. I knew a similar mindset existed at General Motors and that these perceptions were in place when I took the job. Despite the fact that my job was in an uninviting atmosphere, I took it anyway and worked hard to prove the naysayers and doubters wrong.  I got a paycheck which paid my bills.

However, the harassment and alienation I experienced in the job soon showed me that I made a major tradeoff that benefited the company, but did not necessarily benefit me. I worked very long hours in the office and took on difficult projects avoided by my counterparts. I was told later, by a supervisor who valued me as an employee, that I was severely underpaid for my efforts as compared to my white peers. I was often told by sympathetic peers of their upcoming moves to jobs in highly visible parts of the company. But I remained in my hidden role with no one ever suggesting that I look at moving around in the company to win a promotion. It was even publicly suggested by an older white co-worker, at an office lunch outing, that my success was because I was promiscuous. "Hey, Sapphire!"[xli] , a senior white male engineer once yelled to me in front of a group of my co-workers when we went out to lunch together to celebrate the successful conclusion of my projects. I didn't realize what was going on.  A black male co-worker who did immediately pulled the engineer aside and they left the restaurant. After a heated discussion that everyone could see through the restaurant windows, they soon returned and the engineer who greeted me remained silent the rest of the time. It was not until later that I learned the sexual connotations behind what he said and why my black co-worker vocally objected, demanding a public apology on my behalf.  It was just another unfortunate experience added to the list of other negative experiences piling up in a stack. An apology never came from my co-worker. We never mentioned the incident to one another, but the event remained in my memory among others that followed. My experiences working as an engineer were unnecessarily challenging and never easy as wished or hoped.

As the engineer for the chassis department, I was also an engineering supervisor over a handful of skilled trade employees. Skilled trades include carpentry, electrical, metal bending, etc. Most of them were 20 to 30 years older than me with many years of practical work knowledge. All except for one were also white. Their language was salty and their behaviors even saltier. They used curse words like sailors while performing their duties. Pin-up calendars of beautiful women in bikinis perched seductively upon cars and trucks were often posted on their offices. This was their environment and they were proud of it regardless of the fact that women were now entering their workplace. They were okay with women who worked for them and tolerated those women who worked alongside of them. Yet, my situation was different. I was their boss, a black female engineer with a brand new degree who had never done their kind of work in my life.

It was a position that made them unhappy and, boy, did they let me know it through a variety of ways, including work slowdowns in the department or simple refusals to complete the work as I directed. While some of the men immediately accepted me as their co-worker, an equal number did not. The ones who didn't accept me as their supervisor often communicated their thoughts in one-on-one employee review sessions or through angry outbursts at team meetings in front of the entire crew, which added additional stress to a very difficult job.

I was proud to tell others about my job title and levels of responsibility granted to a person of my young age. Behind closed doors, however, this period of my life, the beginning of my STEM journey, was stressful and lonely. After almost two years of working in this difficult environment, my career took off and I began to take more authority and responsibility. This afforded me notoriety within the company and as a leader in the automotive industry.

Years later, when I transitioned from the automotive world and into the health care industry, I was faced with some similar experiences. I made this transition after leaving my executive job at General Motors Corporation and becoming a parental caretaker for two years. I was much older than when I overcame my first hurdle as a newly hired engineer in a manufacturing facility. However the responses and actions of the management in my new career echoed the exact same ones as those of twenty-five years earlier.

I joined a health care non-profit organization in the summer of 2009. It was a highly technical organization focused on information technology software development. The organization was run as if it was a startup. Every person on staff was brought on board because of their technical skills. Despite my history of being an engineering director in one of the largest corporations on the planet, I was treated as a person with much less experience. Even though I acquired new computer programming skills before coming into the job and actually ran a department that built a corporate software application from scratch, I was treated as someone who had very little technical knowledge. I would later learn from one of the consortium member presidents that my vast and "impressive" credentials had been kept secret from them. He did not know the reason for this and was horrified that it happened. "Your job" he said, "was not worthy of your amazing technical talents". These were the same hurdles as almost thirty years before, just in another organization and in another time. This truly angered me.

Considering my years of STEM training, the way I was treated didn't make sense. It was another opportunity for white males to make me "invisible" as I was the only black female engineer forced to sit in a closet-like office away from the main work activities. While complaints were received from the performance of some white males in the organization and I was heralded for my work, my opportunities in the group remained limited while the other individuals continued to rise. Attempts to get help from the Human Resources managers working with the group were met with threats of firing. I did not know that this animosity existed within the organization before I joined it. Nor did I think that this kind of racially and gender-based animosity was still running rampant unmonitored in an area of one of the top colleges within the state of South Carolina. But it was there lurking in the shadows with great force. This environment made my days stressful. The sense of isolation and loneliness in my work environment once again returned.

There were several women at my new employer who acted as my sounding boards and role models. Many of them were either medical doctors or nurses. They expressed equal frustration that the leadership of the health care industry was white-male dominated.

Women and minorities in the field were easily dismissed if they had not achieved some level of name recognition within the medical industry or academia for their clinical discoveries. It is unfortunate and prevents young diverse talent from quickly advancing within the industry.

The few blacks who do make it past the "For Whites Only" signs, who dare sit at the corporate lunch counters are often met with hostility, isolation, and unfair treatment. Bullies who grow from the playground to the workplace do all they can to make the unwanted feel unwelcome. Though most whites in the workplace don't agree with the bullies, the inaction of the silent majority allows the bullies to continue unchecked. The unwillingness of the majority to engage and help protect the vulnerable may be sealing the fate of America. The exclusion of employees because they are "different" means losing creative and brilliant minds.

The Navy employee shared similar experiences and thoughts. "Some of the other employees sympathized with me, but they weren't willing to come forward and confront the bullies. I was on my own. I tried to call the behavior out and filed an EEO complaint. After that, I was ostracized.

"Eventually, it affected my health. I remember dreaming that I was a housemaid for one of the doctors. In the dream, the doctor (who in real life was a supporter of the bullies) was fond of me and liked that I was smart. When I awakened, I realized that he and the others didn't like me because I was out of my position as a black person. My being less made them feel more powerful. But the truth is, the organization made itself weaker by supporting the bullies: I was a really good employee. The bullies that the organization supported were, for the most part, marginal employees. I left. Twenty years later, the complaint I filed is still languishing, unresolved, at the EEOC."

Does this sound familiar? This behavior is not new. It is the same behavior the Greensboro boys met at Woolworths. It is the same behavior that achievers like Venus and Serena Williams have faced. It is the same behavior that talented STEM-trained African Americans of all ages, genders, and levels of authority share stories about on social media platforms like Facebook and Twitter. It is a drain on corporate resources and hobbles the advancement of corporations and start-ups.

My own two experiences taught me one significant lesson about building a career in the STEM world: Be prepared for a lack of positive reception from your co-workers and some supervisors when you start your job. They will not recognize or respect you for the full value of your technical skills and capabilities unless you demand it. Your willingness to accept something less than what you deserve, which was my eventually unsuccessful approach, will advance your career for a while but leave you scarred and bearing a huge personal cost.

With so many companies searching for diverse technical talent, as a black STEMmer, learn to create options for yourself and don't take the first job that comes along. Also, considering hiring yourself and building a tech organization of your own whose environment and culture you control.

Exclusionary corporate culture results in an America that each day exposes its Achilles Heel to the global market. Each time a Chinese investor walks into a corporation, or each time a Middle Eastern investor meets with a corporate board, they view America's vulnerability. What do other global citizens see? They, as people of color, notice the absence of color in America's corporations and board rooms. They know that this phenomena is not natural or happenstance.

At some point, they will exploit this weakness to their advantage. It leaves our nation vulnerable to corporations, and even to terrorist groups who can seduce the vulnerable by simply welcoming the unwanted and offering the glimmer that they will be accepted as human beings.

#BlackLivesMatter is not simply about police brutality. It is also about being humane enough to acknowledge that blacks, like whites, are entitled to employment and self-esteem. Mainstream America, white corporate America, must make room for the black STEM heroes to come—not only at lower levels but also at the highest decision-making levels. They must be welcomed, acknowledged, fairly compensated, rewarded, and promoted.

Corporate diversity managers also have a role to play. They aren't just recruiters, public relations team members, or sideline organizational cheerleaders; their role is to engage leadership to change. When it comes to diversity and inclusion matters, the change can be mountainous. Corporate owners and executives must approach diversity and inclusion from an asset angle, considering, "What new resource and opportunity can be mined to enhance our company and bottom line?" And, "Can this member of my team advance and stabilize my company internationally? Can their different worldview help to enhance mine?"

I recommend that corporate leaders read Black Stem USA, and that they share it with their employees, encouraging them to brainstorm, in small groups, how they might improve their company's diversity and inclusion posture.

If we as a nation are to survive, or if we are to regain global advantage, we must be like the US Army and build a team that does not exclude members or leaders based on race or culture.

Corporations must be honest with themselves about their demographics and how they got that way. They must "get in the game" and make social advancement as important as technological advancement. Simply saying that a company runs on a system of meritocracy is not enough. They must open their doors to team members who do not look like them and who come from different cultures and backgrounds. For the STEM world, this goes beyond opening the doors to Asian and Asian Americans. Corporations must have the wisdom and foresight to see these differences as advantages and strengths. They must step forward and lead.

Inside the STEM culture—just as they would have the courage to be intolerant of those who bully white women or LGBT team members, they must find the courage to stand up against racial bullying. There have to be some whites who are willing to sit at the corporate lunch counter and push back against racial intolerance, like Bob Zellner, a white member of SNCC who risked his life to help others during the first Civil Rights Movement. They must find the courage to identify and wrestle with their own biases and welcome talented "outsiders" to the team.

While in most of my stories I speak of those individuals that worked to hurt my career out of fear, jealousy, and simple racial hatred, I must clarify one thing: There were many more people of all hues, colors, nationalities, genders, ages, sexual orientations, socio-economic statuses, and varying political and religious leanings, that helped me along in my career. I am thankful for the advice, guidance, and comradery that they provided. I would not have gotten as far in my career if sympathetic white males, looking to become future top leaders of their organization, hadn't made the bold move of helping me in some way. White females, Asian-Americans, black males, and many others all helped me in some way.

The help I received came in various forms, from being encouraged to study STEM subjects, to help with the mastery of STEM concepts, to learning the actions to take to become proficient as a STEM worker and then management leader within STEM organizations, to mentorship for the roles that I undertook. There were numerous people whom with I worked that helped me all along the way. I am grateful to all of them wherever they may be.

But the point must be made: It is pointless to send black people into the STEM pipeline unless white corporate America is willing to hire, promote, contract, and welcome blacks to the US STEM team. Without African Americans in the mix, we will become a country increasingly divided. United we stand; divided we fall.

# Chapter 9:
# Black Technology Entrepreneurs

*"Your time is limited, so don't
waste it living someone else's
life. Don't be trapped by dogma
- which is living with the results
of other people's thinking. Don't
let the noise of others' opinions
drown out your own inner
voice. And most important,
have the courage to follow your
heart and intuition."*

~Steve Jobs
Businessman, Entrepreneur

We can control our own destinies.

In 1957, eight young white men met at a restaurant to discuss an idea that would forever change their lives and the future of the world. The men, disgruntled about the negative way in which their supervisor and employer treated them, determined together that they would leave the company and start their own semiconductor venture. It was an atypical move at the time for anyone in the traditional corporate business world and the action carried with it a significant amount of catastrophic risk. Either this group of eight men would soar to the greatest heights of the technology and innovation world or they would bring upon themselves their own personal ruin. Ultimately, together they decided to risk everything and pursue their dream. They changed forever the way we view entrepreneurship.

Signing one-dollar bills as a symbol of commitment to one another and their dream, the men would go on to experience legendary success. They and their innovations led the way to the creation and the formation of a world-changing technology hub called "Silicon Valley" in Southern California.

STEM leaders around the world have sought to copy this group's entrepreneurial strategies and approaches to developing innovations. Becoming an entrepreneur with an innovation that leads to the creation of a technology company is the new prosperity path. In some instances, these efforts have led to similar success levels as those experienced by these eight men. It is important to note, however, that these ventures are high risk. A March 2015 Esquire magazine piece, titled *Friendster: Trials and Errors of a Silicon Valley Serial Entrepreneur*, profiles Jonathan Abrams, the guy who patented the technology for social media. Kent Lindstrom, Abrams' COO at his latest start-up, says "People far overestimate the chances of success from the beginning. You have an idea for a company, and the true odds that it will work out are probably like one in five hundred. Venture capitalists know this. . . .So they're prepared for a large measure of failure. . . . But developers still conduct their lives and their careers in this business as if there's only a 50 percent chance it isn't going to work. I'm being conservative there."

In the article, Abrams added, "Outside of the scale of it, and everyone's expectations, Friendster was just another start-up, one of six or seven I've been involved in. All of them face extraordinarily long odds. Friendster was a good idea, maybe a great idea, and we ran into trouble."

Silicon Valley start-ups are high risk. Of course, with high risk comes the opportunity for high reward and control.

For African-Americans, in particular, the complete story of the initial Silicon Valley entrepreneurs and their subsequent success can be a roadmap towards experiencing its own widespread STEM success. In other words, that is, the creation of an African-American Silicon Valley with a multitude of entrepreneurs building successful technology companies employing large numbers of African Americans working in STEM. Is it possible? Yes.

Is it feasible? The answer to this question lies in understanding the details behind Silicon Valley's enormous effectiveness and the ways in which blacks must work to replicate those details.

Silicon Valley-type success requires the existence of three fundamental elements.

- First, there must be a significant problem or marketable new technology idea around which highly trained and talented people can rally. Call it a Manhattan Project[xlii] or simply a needed action; nonetheless, some type of technology concept is the catalyst.

- Second, there must be an inventive person or team of inventive individuals with an entrepreneurial spirit of risk taking willing to lead the innovation development from an initial concept until it becomes a profitable product in the marketplace.

- Third, there must be an influx of financial capital to fund the development process and activities.

These basic elements are a common three-part recipe. They are the focal point of leadership effort for most technology hubs and entrepreneurial incubators, especially those targeting the black innovation.

However, these three components alone are insufficient to generating widespread and sustainable innovation activity like that of Silicon Valley's startup in the 1950s. A series of secondary elements must be in place for long-term sustainability of a major technology expansion initiative. These elements include and comprise the following:

- Favorable housing and municipal support systems for the individuals working on the technology concept and their families;

- Access to federal contracts which can help advance the research portion in the technology's development, provide a supplemental influx of working capital, and anchor the technology's application within industry;

- Favorable transportation options for the technology workforce so that workers can easily travel to their jobs as the new industry and number of workers grows to support the initiative;

- An organic spinoff process, producing secondary and complimentary companies from the originals that help accelerate the technology field's expansion;

- Educational programs in the local schools in which children of the technology workers receive exposure to new technology concepts and ideas that their parents can help teach and reinforce;

- An artistic communal environment surrounding the technology hub with which the technology workforce can freely interact, be intellectually stimulated, and share ideas; and

- A true meritocracy system rewarding highly talented and productive individuals within the ecosystem for their success and encouraging them to risk and produce more.

These components were outlined clearly in a January 2015 TechCrunch article[xliii], entitled, "East of Palo Alto's Eden: Race and the Formation of Silicon Valley[xliv]". The article reported on the drastic and different outcomes for African Americans located near Silicon Valley who were systematically kept away from the elements outlined above. The result is a community that missed the wave of economic prosperity in the region and is now mired down in poverty as a result.

Similar outcomes can be found in other parts of the country, such as Automation Alley in Detroit, where African-

Americans are not a main fixture in Detroit's rebirth efforts[xlv].

Or, in the nation's capital, Washington, DC, where educational technology companies are creating a new industry[xlvi] of which few African-American entrepreneurs are a part. "It's incredible." a black oil industry consultant shared. "It used to be that Washington, D.C. was the land of milk and honey for African Americans who wanted to make good money with the federal government. Since gentrification started, it's now the place where young white hipster PhDs live. They are starting educational software companies to teach our black kids. But they're not letting us join their companies. It's pretty darn incredible." Instead of leading the technology advancements in these communities making successful advancements, African-American are, once again sidelined, the guinea pigs upon which the technology is tested and built while they are left to continue living in impoverished conditions.

Given the lessons learned from the famous rising of Silicon Valley and the partial focus of current programs to bring and expand black presence in STEM, a black Silicon Valley is possible. It is time to change approaches and seek a comprehensive, holistic, and well-coordinated effort to increase black technology participation and entrepreneurship on a massive and self-sustainable level. This is another important part of black America's collective STEM ambition.

The question remaining is, how does black America use the resources it already has to begin creating its own Silicon Valleys? To answer this question, let us first examine the current effort to increase the number of African American technology workers and entrepreneurs.

*"A mind is a terrible thing to waste"*, was the United Negro College Fund's slogan since its inception in 1972 and the tagline became a memorable piece of the American vernacular. But in 2013, UNCF, as the fund is better known, made an adjustment to this well-known slogan to reflect a shift in the idea of black college success. The new slogan is now *"A mind is a terrible thing to waste, but a wonderful thing to invest in."* According to an interview in the New York Times, UNCF's President Dr. Michael Lomax explained the

organization's advertising campaign change as being a response to the new world that African American college candidates are facing. The new change also reflects a move away from anecdotal comments about the value of investing in young African Americans to a more quantifiable assessment of the investment outcome of donating to UNCF. UNCF has data that now shows that for every $10 invested for the education of an African American in college, there is $102 dollars of return to society from the benefits and contributions that the same individual will later make to society after they graduate. "The new campaign was relevant today", he said, as the United States challenges "itself to compete globally by producing talent. This is not charity any longer. This is an investment in individual students, an investment in our nation's work force, and an investment in retaining our global competitiveness."[xlvii]

This idea of viewing the support of African American college students with donations for college scholarships as a long term and quantifiable investment is a role model example of the different way that black America should organize itself to compete entrepreneurially in the future. In order for blacks to succeed in the new global and technologically advanced economy of the world, a paradigm shift in thinking must immediately take place. Black Americans must think of their collective advancement in today's highly competitive STEM world as a quantifiable financial investment requiring all of the same strategies and tactics used in running investment funds, large corporations, and nimble startups. This means that there needs to be a movement using well-structured financing instruments to fund technology startups by blacks. There needs to be a push for a quantifiable return on every investment made so that future growth in innovation capabilities advances the entire collective. The growth is realized in the form of new businesses and high-paying jobs.

But how does this new approach begin? The first step is to understand the current state of black investment in itself when it comes to STEM-related businesses and determining the changes needed in order for the entire community to be more competitive in the global marketplace.  This is a key step as it then leads to the next one that involves understanding the unique and, perhaps, untraditional strategies that must be undertaken by African Americans to drive improvements in their current self-investing activities as compared to the strategies used by other ethnic groups within the US.

In 2013, the Angel Resource Institute in cooperation with CBInsights, the Angel Capital Association, and the Silicon Valley Bank completed research into the general financing trends of startups within the US. The data showed that for most Americans starting new businesses even in the technology field, the typical infusion of early capital into the startup first comes from the individuals starting the businesses and then their friends and family.  This is called "bootstrapping". After this early commitment of personal capital into starting the venture, then the typical founder or owners seek capital from angel investors and federal contracts (if applicable) before moving on to higher levels of capital infusion from venture capitalists and banks. The underlying assumptions of this type of approach are that the startup founder or entrepreneur has available to him or her discretionary funds to "seed" their business dream and, if the startup founder does not have the initial capital to fund their venture that they can turn to friends and family for help. For African Americans, these may be two false assumptions. Based upon the financial information about wage levels and discretionary funds in the public realm, these two sources of income are virtually non-existent for many blacks. Thus, there is a high probability that this typical model of capital infusion for black entrepreneurs does not apply. Instead, African Americans faced with low to no personal or family income to risk on a startup venture may first seek grants and bank loans then angel investors for their capital. The typical graph of this capital infusion progression looks as follows:

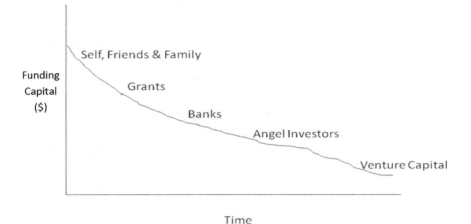

African Americans may also seek venture capital investment earlier time than is typical. This causes outside investors to see them as having greater undesirable risk. It is for this reason that that there is a need for the creation of alternative financial backing strategies to help blacks start STEM businesses if a black Silicon Valley is to exist.

There have been numerous economic reports issued during recent years alerting the public to the fact that the Great Recession of 2007-2009 took a significant financial toll on the African American community, much more so than on other ethnic groups within the country. A 2012 income inequality analysis completed by CNNMoney™ found that while the average net worth of white Americans was $100,000.00, the average African American in the US has a net worth of less than $5,000.00[xlviii] and the majority have liquid wealth[xlix] of only $200.00[l]. This is less money than the amount needed to buy one month's worth of moderately costing groceries in the US[li] and far less than is needed to start a STEM-based company. While one-third of African Americans have $50,000.00 in financial assets from their savings, investments, and employer-sponsored retirement accounts[lii], another 38% of the African American population holds no financial assets, liquid or otherwise.

Of those individuals with student loan debt, African American students (78%) are twice as likely as students of other ethnic groups to carry student debt when graduating from college and the amount owed tends to be higher ($28,692.00)[liii] than that of other ethnic groups. Young college graduates are risk averse to pursuing technology startups when they are facing high levels of debt[liv]. Those graduates that do undertake starting their own companies often struggle with being able to support themselves through the initial ideation phase of a new startup. Dedicated financial resources from blacks must help to alleviate this disadvantage.

African Americans also tend to direct more of their income towards living expenses than to investments or other long term savings instruments which entrepreneurs in other ethnic groups are more able to use.  Black America's wealth has been described as "precarious", "marginal", and "fragile".[lv] The result of this seemingly bleak financial picture is that there is less available capital with which African Americans can individually "bootstrap", or initially self-fund, their business ideas.

In STEM-related fields where an initial infusion of capital can be somewhat higher than in other industry fields, obtaining enough personal funds and capital from family and friends is simply not viable. But there is another part of this story that may offer an alternative picture and strategy upon which change can be built; one involving the coming together of African Americans to collectively target their discretionary funding towards supporting and investing in black technology startups.

While it is true that on an individual basis, black Americans struggle to find the funds to support their entrepreneurial efforts, when looking across the population as a whole, there is more opportunity to fund STEM-related initiatives than is known. A recent online report by Reaching Black Consumers.com shared that in 2014, the average African American black household has approximately $10,000.00 on an annual basis in discretionary income. Black Americans in totality controls $131 billion in discretionary funds and $157 billion[lvi] in discretionary spending surpassing that of Asian Americans and Hispanics[lvii]. Assuming that the average technology company startup requires $750,000.00 to $1,500,000.00 to start viably[lviii], this means that if the African Americans aggregated and funneled just 30% of its available discretionary funds, it would be able to start almost 35,000 technology companies on an annual basis. With the possibility of increasing African American STEM presence in the startup world from only 17% in venture capital-backed early stage technology teams[lix] to 35,000 per year, it is clear that blacks must come together and take a different approach to building its STEM business pipeline than it is currently and has in the past.

For most African Americans in STEM, local banks, grants, or government contracts are the primary initial source of income for their business startups. In recent years, however, due to the tightening of credit in the financial banking system, the reduction of grants due to the government budget downsizing, and the elimination of set asides in many states for minority and women businesses, the available capital from these sources for business startups has also become a non-viable option for many African Americans wishing to start companies. This state is especially true for those seeking to start STEM-related operations.

These discretionary spending funds might be pooled through national or local organizations. They also might be collected through churches, some of which have already established credit unions.

Finally, two other capital infusion mismatches adversely affecting African Americans exist in the angel investor and venture capital realm. One has to do with investors and the other with geography.

There are relatively few African American individuals who have accumulated the required levels of wealth or are making the required level of income to qualify as angel investors able to invest in technology startups.

The SEC defines a "qualified" angel investor as an individual who has over $500,000.00 of net worth in liquidity or who is earning an income exceeding $250,000.00 on an annual basis. These two limits cancel out many African Americans from qualifying as angel investors. Because the population of black angel investor is smaller, the opportunity for a black STEM entrepreneur to be funded by one is also decreased.

Additionally, many of the venture capital firms in the country with money to fund STEM-related startups are located in the Northeastern and Western portions of the United States. These capital hubs are centered primarily in Silicon Valley in the San Francisco-Palo Alto corridor of California and the Silicon Alley corridor that lies from Boston, Massachusetts to New York City, NY. These two regions, while accessible to large portions of the African Americans virtually, are physically far removed from where much of the African American population resides and are educated, particularly those attending HBCUs.

In the 1990s, African Americans made a mini-migration back to the southern region of the United States. The states of Florida and Georgia experienced the largest portion of Black America's southern migration while all other areas of the country (i.e. the northeast, Midwest, and west) saw declines in their black populations[ix]. Orlando, Florida, and Atlanta, Georgia, became modern-day American black metropolises. This migration pattern moved blacks away from the future major sources of technology-focused venture capital in the

country in the 2000s. The effects of the Great Recession

experienced by the country in the mid-2000s further

exacerbated the geographical anchor of African Americans to

the southeastern region due to the economic devastation

experienced, in particular, by blacks. Reduction in their home

ownership wealth and the trend of companies to not offer

relocation money with job offers are preventing many of them

from moving to locations of greater financial advantage[lxi].

This mismatch in African American residential locations

and financing hubs for tech companies during one of the

significant growth periods in the country has made it even

harder for new African American technology startups. Data

from the 2013 Harbor Report shows that only 9% of all US

venture capital funding groups and their $8.369 billion

available to invest in startups and technology companies exist

in the south, including the state of Texas.

The geographical mismatch of angel investors and

venture capital firms away from the majority of the black

people in the country further exacerbates the problem of African Americans' abilities to not only start successful technology companies, but to grow them and sustain them as viable entities in the later stages of development.

A 2010 study by Harvard University found that entrepreneurial business ventures receiving funding from angel investors have a higher rate of continued success and growth into larger businesses than startups without this type of financial support[lxii]. This determination was made after reviewing the progress of 2,600 business ventures that sought angel investment support. Those business ventures receiving support overwhelmingly outperformed those ventures that sought angel investment support and were declined. The study's data suggests that the reason for this superior performance was due to the review activity the business proposals underwent prior to receiving their initial funds, the funds provided, and the mentorship provided by the angel investors as part of the financing deal.

With African Americans living physically in locations of the country where angel investor and venture capital activity and support is lower, the opportunity for technology startups within the country is severely hampered and may explain the reason why initiatives to increase the number of blacks starting successful technology businesses have had limited results.

These two limiters present a major problem. In order for African Americans to obtain the necessary funding needed to kickoff technology companies, alternative approaches must be immediately undertaken. Rather than looking to the western and northeastern regions of the US for startup financing support, a new hub of entrepreneurial activity needs to be created closer to where more African Americans are geographically located and where more financing resources controlled by blacks are also located. Creating a technology hub in Atlanta, Georgia, one of the cities with a large black population or in my hometown, Durham, NC near the Research Triangle Park, (one of the five most STEM-intensive business communities in the Mid-Atlantic region) and with some of the most research-funded HBCUs, MSIs, black banks, and black investment firms could be the answer. Naming the hub, "Silicon Fields"[lxiii], presents an ambitious opportunity to build a powerful black southeastern counterpart to Silicon Valley and Silicon Alley.  Atlanta and Durham are also geographically located within ideal travel distance for individuals from the Deep South, Midwest, Mid-Atlantic, and Southwest regions who wish to interact with the hub.

This African American focused entrepreneurial STEM hub concept with supportive policies in a centralized location with access to technology ideas, human and much-needed financial capital will require a new paradigm in thinking. And that paradigm shift will require other modifications in business approaches and thinking from those used by African Americans today.

# Chapter 10:
# Black Crowdfunding

*"If you want to go quickly,*
*go alone. If you want to go*
*far, go together."*
~African Proverb

The idea of starting a STEM business seems like a daunting dream. The idea of a black person starting a STEM company, given all of the economic issues that hinder it, as discussed in the previous chapter, requires believing in miracles. I know. I've tried more than once to start a company and it is a formidable task. There's almost nothing more humbling than having a technology innovation idea, completing your research and preparing your business plan, only to discover that obtaining the capital to make it happen is next to impossible. However, there are new tools becoming available that piggy backs on how other ethnic communities raise cash to support their STEM dreams and how African Americans did it in the past. "Crowdfunding" is one of the key new tools.

The approach is exploding in its usage by technology entrepreneurial groups across the country. These groups usually do not include black STEM entrepreneurs among their ranks. Given the need to increase African American participation in the long term prosperity that comes from STEM-related initiatives, this lack of black representation in the crowdfunding world must change. This is a key tool for use in the STEM civil rights movement.

Several years ago, an instructor of mine addressed the class I was attending. "There are various ways in which entrepreneurs can obtain funding these days. The traditional ways are with angel investors and venture capital groups. However, there is a new way of getting investors called 'crowdfunding'. What do you folks think about this?"

Several hands went up as I looked around the room full of technology entrepreneurs and wannabe investors that had assembled for a day of investment tutelage sponsored by the South Carolina Chamber of Commerce. There was an impressive group of individuals in the room. Many of them were entrepreneurs already experiencing initial success with their software startups. Some were also already through their first round of seed funding. These same individuals were there to meet potential investors for their second round of funding and were not shy about their thoughts on the crowdfunding topic. "I wouldn't want to get involved with it," said one eager young female entrepreneur. "I don't want 'uneducated' people involved with making decisions about my company," she elaborated. "I want people who understand what investing in a company means and have the knowledge to help me." I looked around the room to see if her comments bothered anyone else besides me. Sadly, I concluded that I was the sole person in the room who seemed unsettled by her comments.

The young lady continued, "I also don't want to be involved with people who can't afford to loan this money because they need it to pay their everyday bills, nor do I want to have someone try to sue me because something unexpected went wrong with my startup and these people lost money that they could not afford to lose. I want educated and qualified investors involved with my company, if at all possible, and if I am not absolutely desperate. So on the subject of crowdfunding, I am going to take a pass." As the young woman was speaking, I once again scanned the room to observe my classmate's responses. The numerous heads nodding around the conference room table gave a clear indication that this was the popular position of many in attendance; the option of crowdfunding was something to be avoided at all costs; only in desperation should the option be considered. At the time, for this group of mostly white entrepreneurs and investors, it was an open and shut case. But for the majority of African Americans, where personal bootstrapping funds and seed round capital are not readily available, even though they are desperately needed, the crowdfunding option may be the only reasonable option in the near term to rapidly enable and expand the black STEM research and business opportunities.

Now, two years later, there's been a revolution in white entrepreneurial attitudes toward the crowdfunding concept: the concept is fully embraced. However, many black Americans are still unaware or leery of the concept. This results in the lack of funding for STEM startups by the black community. The option of a large group of interested individuals as a possible funding source needs to be more closely examined by African Americans before it can be so easily, and incorrectly, dismissed.

Crowdfunding is an old dog with new virtual tricks. According to the website, Investopedia, crowdfunding is the collection of small amounts of capital from a wide array of individuals to finance a business venture, philanthropic or creative project. A pre-virtual world example of crowdfunding in the African American history is the "Harlem house-rent parties" of the 1920s and 30s[lxiv]. At these events, "invited" individuals attending the party would "pay" a few dollars to the host of the party for the opportunity to attend the party as part of a neighborhood effort to help pay a neighbor's apartment rent to prevent their eviction. The accumulated money from all of the party attendees was used to pay the rent of the host without any transfer of rental rights to those who help provided the capital. "Crowdfunding" African-American rents back then was widely done in Harlem, New York due to the high rents charged to live in this black Mecca of the early 19th century, but the concept spread and was used in other cities. The money collected from rent parties became a self-funded tool that the struggling blacks used to help each other overcome the financial trouble they faced. The new trick is that the collection is done online.

Today's crowdfunding avenues are similar in concept to the rent parties of the past; money is collected from various interested individuals seeking to financially support other individuals of entrepreneurial pursuits and given to the party of interest to help them get their business or project started. It was understood in these money exchanges of the past that while the money was "donated" to help pay the rent of the host, there was no legal obligation on the behalf of the host to share their home with those who provided them with money. This arrangement is similar to modern crowdfunding activities. However, whereas the Harlem rent-parties, were purely a purview of the black community, crowdfunding is now used by mainstream society to help fund philanthropic endeavors (i.e. donation-based funding) and make initial investments in business startups (i.e. investment crowdfunding) of all types. The capital raising option is becoming more widespread amongst white entrepreneurs and is a viable, yet still cautionary, option.

To understand crowdfunding further and the way in which blacks can use this strategy to increase their start of technology companies, let's look deeper. There are four types of crowdfunding options for startups; rewards-based, donations-based, equity-based, and debt-based. Rewards-based crowdfunding or the "goodie bag" funding scenario involves using crowdfunding Internet platforms like Kickstarter and Indiegogo to obtain money from investors and, in return, giving the investors non-monetary goodwill "rewards" for their "investment". The second type of crowdfunding is donation-based and involves using online platforms such as Crowdrise and Gofundme to get financial donations made from the general public for philanthropic and charitable projects. Neither rewards-based nor donations-based crowdfunding provide the investor with benefit of partial ownership in the project or company they are supporting.

Equity-based crowdfunding platforms, like EarlyShares, AngelList, and Crowdfunder are the third option and it allows certain individuals with greater discretionary wealth[lxv] to invest small portions of their money into companies with an expected rate of return. Investors own a small ownership interest in the business they are funding. A complete list of equity-based crowdfunding sites is provided in the bibliography of this document.

The last type of crowdfunding is debt-based and is more generally known, as peer-to-peer microlending. Similar to the equity-based crowdfunding option, investors are guaranteed a specified rate of return and also receive a stake within the company. This type of crowdfunding occurs with Internet sites like Kiva, Prosper, and Lending Club.

According to an excerpt of a Massolution® report[lxvi] as reported by journalist Chance Barnett in Forbes magazine[lxvii], in 2012 the crowdfunding industry had grown to $2.7 billion with a projected growth to $5.1 billion in 2013. The United States, the largest crowdfunding market, was at a $1.6 billion level in 2012. In 2012, this funding level helped one million individual campaigns spread from across the globe. Massolution's latest report indicates that there is still room in the crowdfunding space for new entrants even as the industry is maturing. Well-known donation and rewards-based[lxviii] funding sites such as Kickstarter and Indiegogo, and investment funding sites such as Crowdfunder (for startups), Somolend (for mature young companies seeking later stage funding), and Quirky (for inventors) are the cornerstones of the maturing industry, but these groups tend not to adequately service the underserved (i.e. African Americans among others) and niche portions of society. Initial forays into black crowdfunding, like BlackStartup.com and BlackStartup.net were unsuccessful. Comparatively, a Latino crowdfunder, Crowdismo now called Align Capital, has taken off and is doing well. The lack of black crowdfunding activity, if handled the right way, provides a golden opportunity for well-organized niche technology startup platforms designed specifically for the black community.

What can be achieved by funding black technology startups through a crowdfunding platform? Let's take a look at the crowdfunding platform, Kickstarter, as an example. Kickstarter, alone, is now at $1 billion in total pledged investment dollars from almost 6 million people acting as investors[lxix]. The Kickstarter investors come from over 218 countries and territories with the majority of the investors in the US. The crowdfunding site reports that over $1 million is contributed to the projects housed on their site every single day[lxx]. That is over $694.00 pledged every minute of every single day! Where are these investors coming from? Over half of Kickstarter investors make on average less than

$50,000.00 per year, slightly lower than the average income within the US, and yet many of these individuals are participating in successful investment opportunities with little to no difficulty or adverse outcome[lxxi]. However, African American participation in this type of investment activity is far below other ethnic groups and at only 4% of Kickstarter's investor population[lxxii]. Imagine the possibilities if more blacks participated in crowdfunding.

With greater investor education and exposure within black circles and training through targeted outreach on how to use these easily available Internet-based tools, the crowdfunding approach could become one of the significantly viable and widespread investment options for startup STEM companies with which the African American community can build its technology prowess. Examples of the potential success that could be garnered from this investment approach can be found with the Kickstarter campaigns of Spike Lee and LeVar Burton. Spike Lee, a famous independent and Academy Award-nominated black filmmaker, used Kickstarter to raise funds for two independent films that he wished to produce and direct. His controversial 2013 campaign, with an original investment goal of $1.25 million, raised over $1.4 million with 6,421 investors. LeVar Burton, a well-known black actor, made Kickstarter history for raising money to revive and provide access to the children's TV show, "*Reading Rainbow*", through the expansion of software application for computer tablets. LeVar also exceeded his original $1 million investment goal and raised over $3.5 million. In telling the story behind the impetus for using the Kickstarter platform, Mr. Burton stated that traditional venture capital groups refused to fund the project and could not see the vision of the market for the product[lxxiii]. He and his team were so convinced that today's children needed the Reading Rainbow app that they would not take "no" for an answer and turned to crowdfunding to make their dream come true. The successful 35-day campaign ended with 75,000 investors with the average contribution below $45.00. While both of these examples are creative arts projects, the same level of success is possible for black technology projects needing investment funding.

What concerns could be holding back African Americans from jumping eagerly into crowdfunding? The risk of losing an investor's capital is greater with equity and debt crowdfunding than with the rewards- and donation-based versions. For African Americans with little discretionary money and limited lifetime savings to startup technical businesses, the risks associated with participating in crowdfunding investment activities can be high and may not be immediately attractive. However, recent federal legislation containing SEC protective limits on crowdfunding as outlined in the Crowdfund Provision of the 2012 JOBS Act and the implementation by state governments of a second layer protective laws for crowdfunding participants could help alleviate concerns in this regard.

The maximum money that can be "gathered" by an entrepreneur through a crowdfunding website, per new US legislation, is $1 million within a 12-month period. This is the typical amount of STEM-related or technology startup capital needed in the more traditional seed funding setting of accredited angel investors and venture capital groups. The JOBS Act requires audited financial statements once the amount collected from the crowdfunding campaign totals half a million dollars. The law also makes it easier for successful companies to issue initial public offerings of stock in their entities, and enables entrepreneurs to advertise and solicit wealth investors to invest in their companies. In other words, the equity crowdfunding of today is the modern day legal, SEC-regulated virtual version of yesterday's Harlem house-rent party for blacks. It is a tool that African Americans can use in the STEM movement strategy.

The crowdfunding concept is an ideal solution for individuals in which racial discrimination and aspects of their personal hurdles (e.g. limited credit, limited personal financial resources, etc.) prevent them from receiving traditional business startup financing and where the African American community, as a whole, is limited by its reduced net worth as to the amount it has available to support a major initiative to build its STEM-related business capabilities. While the SEC and state regulations associated with the JOBS Act may appear to be restrictive, the rules used in the right way will help protect African Americans from suffering fraud and bankruptcy by preventing any financial bubbles from this type of activity.

For American business, concerns about and high rates of exposure to fraud by African Americans[lxxiv] are barriers to the black community's crowdfunding inclusion. I, myself, sometimes carry this same personal bias. The concerns increase when the business interaction is virtual by nature. It is an unfair bias that must be overcome with the creation of successful crowdfunded black technology startups.

Current crowdfunding fraud across the industry is low and almost non-existent. A study by Wharton Business School Professor Ethan Mollick at the University of Pennsylvania[lxxv] found that out of almost 2100 US-based projects involving $237 million on Kickstarter only $21,324.00 had been lost by investors. This represents a fraud level of almost 0%; an unbelievably low risk rate given the nature of crowdfunding where investors do not, generally, meet the leaders of the ventures in which they are investing. Dr. Mollick partially attributes this low fraud rate to the concept of the "wisdom of the crowd" in that the multitude of objective third-parties assessing the information presented act in a similar fashion to a group of well-versed angel investors.

Most projects experience no fraud due to the legal ramifications of not fulfilling the promises made to investors. Unfortunately, one such failed crowdfunding startup by a black individual who jumped into crowdfunding early has unfairly caused scrutiny of other black projects. Seth Quest, a black entrepreneur, who raised $35,000.00 on Kickstarter to produce a new iPad stand called the Hanfree, failed to deliver the product to the market[lxxvi]. In response, he was sued by his Kickstarter investors and became bankrupt. When looking into the details of the causes behind Seth's failure, it turns out the problem was not his idea; the idea was solid and had great promise. Unfortunately, Seth had not been coached on making sure manufacturers were contractually ready to produce when his crowdfunding campaign concluded. This lack of preparation caused him difficulties in getting anyone to manufacture the product with the funds that he raised. If Seth had received expert guidance or attracted a business mentor to help him in this entrepreneurial venture, this failure might not have come about and a fraud lawsuit avoided. Also, if the investors who provided him with the initial seed money through Kickstarter had been provided more details about Seth's plan for executing the Hanfree product as is done in other Kickstarter projects, their collective assessment might have been that his product manufacturing plans were lacking and avoided investing in his campaign. The Hanfree debacle and others like it may be the reason that technology product projects are now formally scrutinized before their promotion is allowed on the crowdfunding site.[lxxvii] This filter for fraudulent projects is critical financially and culturally for African Americans. While the Hanfree disaster may make some concerned about investing online in black technology businesses, it is important to note that few, if any, similar crowdfunding washouts have occurred since.

Surprisingly, suspicion of black businesses is also a concealed concern for African Americans. Many blacks have lost money in the past by trusting honest (and unlucky) and dishonest (or truly fraudulent) business owners in their community. It is a real and ever present danger. Let's discuss this further.

Fraud is serious concern for many African Americans who live in neighborhoods in which large numbers of people are "getting their hustle on" as part of an effort to improve their financial situations. Fraud is a concern of mine. Fraud is real and, in the age of the Internet and cybercrimes, it is happening more frequently. I am sad to report that I experienced fraud from people I knew well and didn't know well. People who were black and people who were not. I've lost lots of money from unknowingly doing business with fraudsters. One time I lost money, tens of thousands of dollars, in a legitimate franchise deal because the company advertised that they provided a service to support me as a franchisee, but the service really didn't exist. A clear case of fraud. Another time, I lost money doing business with an executive recruiting company. The company was legitimate, however the person who was my assigned coach did things that were not. This was another case, in my mind, of fraud. A third time, I was robbed of money from an Internet contact who claimed to need temporary help with his business, and who faked romantic intentions. This was a deeply painful way for me to, yet again, be a fraud victim.

Fraud can happen anywhere, any time, and with anyone. It can strip you of money you've worked your whole life to save. It is a terrible thing. But it is not a black or white racial problem; it is a poor character issue. The correct response to fraud is not to refuse to embrace new business ideas such as crowdfunding. Instead, the lesson is to learn the characteristics of fraudsters, become familiar with the tools of fraud protection, and trust your gut when a business opportunity seems too good to be true. Don't give up on your dreams of owning your own tech business because of someone else's poor character. You may miss a legitimate opportunity to help a million dollar black business idea become reality. Making African Americans more prosperous through STEM careers and technology business outweighs the risk involved. It is our collective wisdom and experiences which will protect against fraudulent schemes. However, before we can talk about protecting ourselves, more blacks need to jump into the crowdfunding pool.

Bottom-line – crowdfunding fraud is an anomaly on both the side of the individual initiating the crowdfunding campaign and the people who invest. It is a worthwhile and necessary tool that can help African Americans grow its portfolio of STEM-related business and population of technology entrepreneurs. With greater and widespread education about making effective investments, this type of investor fraud should not increase to any significant level. And if there remains a concern about the wisdom of the crowd not protecting black Americans, additional actions could be undertaken. Actions, such as creating avenues to provide insurance for crowdfunding fraud risk, accelerating training and using crowdfunding educational tools, and lobbying for policies requiring crowdfunding sites to supply more information about the proposer's background are options to consider.

The use of crowdfunding to help black America grow its business presence in the universe of technology startups should be thoughtfully considered and strategically applied. Strategies to mitigate the risk of fraudulent STEM-related and technology startup business proposals will have to be devised and their effectiveness closely monitored going forward to ensure that its financial interests are not preyed upon, but protected.

White Americans have moved beyond the distrust I observed in that South Carolina crowdfunding meeting just a couple of years ago. It is time for the black collective with a strategic focus on building a black STEM investment fortress to do the same.

# Chapter 11:
# Black STEM and the Media

*"The people who influence
you are the people who
believe in you."*

~Henry Drummond,
Scottish Evangelist and Writer

How can African Americans begin to create a sense of urgency around the issue of creating a black STEM civil rights movement? A tried and true tool should be used; the black media. Black America has always enjoyed a unique and rich historical ability of spreading important information throughout its community via different communication methods since the first Africans were brought to America. Increased black media ownership and participation over the last fifty years has helped the sharing of critical information. From newspapers to magazines (like Ebony, Essence, and Jet), to Afro-centric movies, radio shows, and TV networks, blacks have used media to communicate, inform, and rally themselves around issues of vast importance. This use of media is finding its way into the dialogue about black alienation in the world of STEM.

Black researchers, like Dr. Kevin Clark, PhD.[lxxviii] , the Director

and Founder of George Mason University's Center for Digital

Media, Innovation and Diversity, are being recognized for their

work to understand how blacks relate to digital media

platforms in an effort to garner more interest in technology.

Black Enterprise magazine not only regularly highlights black

advancements and opportunities in the finance and general

business world, but now provides added emphasis on STEM

and technology-related careers and business opportunities

within its editions and its Meet the Tech Titans events at its

Black Enterprise Entrepreneurs Conferences. Ebony

magazine has the STEM All-Stars awards in partnership with

the US Whitehouse. Local efforts such as Bowie, Maryland's

public TV access show called "The Launch Pad" by nonprofit

The Pursuing A Dream Corporation are working to make

information about local African American technology activities

more accessible. Additionally, the CNN show Black In

America: The Promised Land hosted by Soledad O'Brien, a

well-respected black investigative reporter and former CNN

news anchor, introduced several African American technology

entrepreneurs and the black-focused technology startup incubator, NewMe, to the general American audience. In the segment, data regarding the absence of significant black presence in the technology companies located in Silicon Valley was presented. Media-based outreach to bolster black STEM interest includes the use of social media. NPR, the National Public Radio, has held Twitter events with black audiences on the topic of STEM and technology participation. NPR's "Tell Me More" Twitter series and *#NPRBlacksinTech's* "A Day in the Life" series provides opportunities for African American Twitter users to communicate real-time with successful black technologists.

When performing a combined Google search on the words "African American", "media", and "STEM", over 19 ½ million results are returned. Most of the information provided show that there is a concentrated effort occurring across the country to interest African American children in the STEM fields. However, there is less evidence that a strategic media plan exists for consistent outreach to all pipeline portions around the issue STEM participation. One is needed and if it is to be created, it must be highly strategic and entertaining to be effective.

Successful media messaging requires three primary things to be considered; the message's content, placement, and frequency. When these three parameters are considered, a well-formulated media activity can have an impactful and lasting effect on the audience it is targeting.

A strategic approach to increasing media content about black STEM must also include consideration of the fact that for many people science is not a subject that is easy to understand or of great interest. "In communicating information about science-related items to the public, it must be constructed in a way to draw people's interest and people, generally, are not interested in science."[lxxix] This is especially true in the social media sphere of Twitter. As mentioned earlier, younger African Americans have a propensity to use Twitter, a real-time avenue for having discussions around topics of communal interest. Unfortunately, recent studies have also shown that these interest areas are primarily with celebrity gossip and entertainment news[lxxx]. While this social media platform is a tool that could be of great advantage for African Americans in building its STEM prowess through activities like crowdfunding and Twitter chats, it will not become this if a concerted and concentrated effort is not made. Just as a paradigm shift is needed in the way in which the black community is approaching its participation in STEM-related careers and formulating its own technology companies, a comprehensive and holistic approach needs to be undertaken in the black media approach around this subject.

Using such media drawers as Dr. Neil DeGrasse-Tyson, the Cosmos TV show host, and Morgan Freeman, the host of Through the Wormhole, would go a long way to make science interesting and fun for the average black media consumer. Following Shonda Rhimes' lead with the hit television shows, Grey's Anatomy and Private Practice(defunct), more black –centric shows like ABC's

(American Broadcasting Company) Scandal and 'black•*ish*, and Fox's Empire and Rosewood need to infuse themselves with STEM savvy black characters that are aspirational. Other shows, should strive to contain STEM savvy black characters in their storylines a well.

As African Americans show a propensity to be enamored with celebrities in sports and the entertainment industry, highlighting individuals in those two industries that are using innovative technology and forming STEM-related businesses could help garner wider STEM interest. Similar work to the TV series "Black in America", more documentaries on tech savvy individuals such as music artists Will.i.am, Dr. Dre, and comedian Baratunde Thurston need to be created and shown on networks with high black audiences.

Earlier chapters of this book contain discussions about Will.i.am and Dr. Dre's tech efforts. Baratunde Thurston attacks the black tech issue from a different viewpoint. Combining comedy with technology, the New York Times Best Selling author and tech entrepreneur, recently led the merger of his business with an up and coming San Francisco high tech design company. His newly expanded company will be creating digital content for the 100Kin10 initiative[lxxxi]. A heavy Twitter engager, Baratunde (twitter handle: *@baratunde*) also helps to spread the ideas of increased African American engagement in STEM fields in a way that is readily accepted by youth.

These entertainers and their stories need to be more broadly communicated to the black public at-large. As known role models for many young African Americans, these individuals can show that blacks can be wildly successful on the level of Steve Jobs (the founder of Apple), Mark Zuckerberg (the founder of Facebook) or Jack Dorsey (the founder of Twitter and Square) in STEM–related endeavors where they are at the helm.

The black media can also use its entertainment platform to familiarize African Americans with iconic tech events by showcasing African American STEM entrepreneurs discussing their endeavors at such events as SXSW and Las

Vegas' Consumer Electronics Show, more commonly referred to by the acronym CES. Highlighting the exciting portions of these events on black network TV and radio shows would help expose young African Americans to the exciting tech opportunities that await them around the country. Black networks can also help bolster K-12 interest by showing African American participants in the National Science Fair held at the Whitehouse and the National Science Festival held on the National Mall in Washington, DC. Shows, including cartoons, with excited black youth and others of varying ages would help expose children to STEM in an entertainment medium of which they are already heavy users[lxxxii].

There are so many ways in which the black media, entertainers, and celebrities can spread the message that blacks need to start participating in STEM. The industry has the tools, the celebrities, and the access to make the story exciting and compelling. These assets should be part of any integral plan to communicate more STEM information to black Americans.

# Chapter 12: "Stay Gold" - WE Are Our Answer

*"What lies behind us and
what lies ahead of us are
tiny matters compared to
what lives within us."*

> ~Henry David Thoreau, American Author, Poet,
> Philosopher, Abolitionist

*"Change will not come if
we wait for some other
person or some other
time. We are the ones
we've been waiting for.
We are the change that
we seek."*

> ~ President Barrack Hussein Obama
> 44th and 1st African-American President
> United States of America

One of the most popular and exciting movie genres is

films on the American West. The films usually contain exciting

stories of early Americans who took all their families and

belongings and moved to the untamed and little developed

western part of the country. "There's gold in them there hills",

is often the rallying cry as the actors play the settlers looking to make significant economic gains from the wealth that lay deep within the land.

For African Americans and their need to increase their technology business acumen, this needs to become the rallying cry. There's gold in the hills of STEM and technology innovation and a targeted holistic plan to move the whole community towards this gold must be started today. African Americans have a history of accomplishing major goals when their efforts are focused and coordinated. The Civil Rights Movement of the twentieth century is contemporary proof. This technology movement of the 21st century can be achieved in a similar way.

The movement will require greater recognition that African Americans, despite their current socio-economic predicaments, do have a magnitude of resources whose use is presently not maximized. A better understanding and communication of these resources will help the community see positively that its technology ambitions can be achieved. Black America also needs to leverage the educational resources at its disposal as a way to jumpstart its foray on a massive scale. HBCUs and MSIs, with their research and ethnically-focused missions, must help lead the way towards increased STEM innovations and STEM-trained workers to help accelerate the rate of black activity in this new sector. There needs to be greater coordination between all parts of black ecosystem to better leverage the efforts that are currently underway within the community. Black researchers, investors, banking institutions, entrepreneurs, incubators, and educators, entertainers, and media leaders need to come together under one centralized consortium to build a plan together that will enable the whole community to move towards STEM in a coordinated and high-impact way. Efforts that generate significant positive results need to be analyzed and disseminated on a wider basis. Activities that are not generating positive results need to be stopped.

Coordinated efforts with individuals, groups, and organizations external to the black community need to be formally sought and fully developed to help every aspect along the entire pipeline of the black STEM initiative. The establishment of a hub in the southern portion of the US would help to geographically center the African American efforts associated with a STEM movement within the middle of the geographic location where most of them live. There are many technology companies, PWIs, and federal agencies actively seeking to help black America grow its presence in the technology industry. These highly engaged resources should continue to be heavily leveraged.

Individuals, of all ages, need to be made more aware of the opportunities in STEM in such a way that they seek out training in the technology fields. TV and radio mediums should be used for delivering a consistent and continuous message on a broad scale about black technology and the wealth streams from it. The young black community's use of social media should be exploited so that they are constantly seeing information about STEM opportunities presented to them in an engaging format to help promote the benefits of becoming a black STEMmer that may not be easily seen.

Black entrepreneurs must be given new financing approaches that are better suited to the financial realities they face as members of the African American community. Black investors and banking institutions must play a more active and visible role in helping to support and fund startup businesses in technology.  Methods of obtaining startup funds for technology companies through new funding strategies such as crowdfunding, social impact bonds, and donor-advised funds need to be explored and employed. Successful uses of these new approaches need to be communicated throughout the entire community so that it will foster more individuals to follow. The execution of a 21st century Civil Rights movement around STEM and technology would advance the entire community.

Economic success in the US is no longer based on manual labor as it was with the agriculture and Industrial Revolution periods. Modern success and competitive advancement in the future will be built around the ability to create and use technology. For the US to remain a global superpower, all its people must embrace and become a part of the technology revolution. African Americans have remained outside of this sea of change and are suffering economic shortcomings as a consequence. Black America must roll up its sleeves and welcome all to join in this battle if we as a whole are to survive.

While the current picture of black America's missing-in-action status as producers of advanced technology in the innovation and knowledge-based world presents an alarming red flag, it is important to note that this is only a partial picture. The technology race is still underway and with a more concentrated focus, better use of available resources and a comprehensive work effort (i.e. a new civil rights movement 2.0), the African-American technology involvement picture can be completely altered and changed.

News flash! It may not be widely known, but African-Americans already possess everything needed to radically turn things around for the better. Indeed, we possess enough as a population to make everything a *great* deal better. To do this, it will require becoming different and learning more empowering facts about the status of our community. We must creatively analyze the ways in which past tools and concepts, used when our community was faced with similar trials, can be modernized; intentionally embracing a different mindset by joining and supporting grassroots efforts. Finally, we must seek out appropriate media and close our ears to the current media messages that seek to convince us that we do not have the capability to overcome our present technology participation lag, that whisper to us that we are not welcome and do not belong.

All of this *can* be done. These are not pie-in-the-sky statements.

They are fact.

A change in the way in which Black America engages with the technology and innovation portions of modern day society is undeniably needed. The steps to bring about that change can begin with the information included in this book.

Ready or not, it's time for a change.

The change MUST begin now!

Until we have won the technology race, we should not rest.

More of us *can* be seated at the world's table of prosperity.

With black STEM, we CAN be the best.

**C.M. Williams**, a North Carolina native, was on the corporate frontlines at General Motors when a Black in Detroit's boardrooms was a rare idea. A former executive in GM's Product Development Division, Williams was part of the Chevy Volt Original Concept Team, and was recently appointed to South Carolina's Consumer Protection/Medical Liability Subcommittee by Governor Nikki Haley and is founder of C M Williams & Associates, LLC, a boutique consulting, data analytics, and publishing company. For more information visit www.cmwilliamsandassociates.com.

Co-author **Sharon Ewell Foster** is best known for her critically-acclaimed, bestselling, and award-winning historical fiction. Her first novel, *Passing by Samaria* (Multnomah), was named the NAACP Book of the Year in 2000 and won the Christy Award for Fiction. Her most recent novel, *The Resurrection of Nat Turner (Parts I and II)* (Simon and Schuster) is winner of the Civil War Institute's 2012 Shaara Prize for Best Civil War Fiction. Ms. Foster's first publication was a repair manual for the U.S. Army's Pershing 1a Missile System Black Deflector. She has twenty years' experience as a technical writer, logistician, analyst and instructor. For more information, and to learn about her other books, visit www.officialsharonewellfoster.com

# www.blackstemusa.com

# Endnotes

This section contains the source material used in the creation of this book. Thank you to all the individuals and organizations who completed the research that assisted with the formulation of ideas and proposals articulated in this book.

---

[i] Landivar, Liana Christin, "Disparities in STEM Employment by Sex, Race, and Hispanic Origin". US Census Bureau, Washington, D.C., September 2013. Pages 1-25.

[ii] Mississippi Black Code. https://chnm.gmu.edu/courses/122/recon/code.html.

[iii] The Rise and Fall of Jim Crow. Jim Crow Stories. www.PBS.org.

[iv] Dyer Anti-Lynching Bill. www.wikipedia.org. https://en.wikipedia.org/wiki/Dyer_Anti-Lynching_Bill.

[v] "United Artists Corporation, It's a Mad Mad Mad Mad World", 1963.

[vi] During the editing phase of this book, Google announced this change in its company structure. The update was added to the book.

[vii] International Labour Office. "A Skilled Workforce for Strong, Sustainable and Balanced Growth: A G20 Training Strategy". Geneva, 2010. Pages 1-41.

[viii] Office of the Secretary. United States Department of Labor. "Futurework – Trends and Challenges for Work in the 21st Century", 1999.

[ix] National Academies of Science Annual Meeting. Remarks by President Barrack Obama speech. Washington, D.C., April 27, 2009.

[x] Thibodeau, Patrick and Maclis, Sharon, "With H1-B Visas, Diversity Doesn't Apply". Computerworld, August 10, 2015.

[xi] Malcolm Gladwell. David and Goliath: Underdogs, Misfits, and the Art of Battling Giants. Little, Brown, and Company, 2013.

[xii] Harris Interactive, "STEM Perceptions: Student & Parent Study, Parents and Students Weigh In on How To Inspire The Next Generation of Doctors, Scientists, Software Developers, and Engineers".

[xiii] Locke, Edward, "Proposed Model for A Streamlined, Cohesive, and Optimized K-12 STEM Curriculum with a Focus on Engineering". The Journal of Technology Studies, Volume 35, Number 2, Winter 2009.

[xiv] National Action Council on Minorities in Engineering, Inc. Research & Policy, "African Americans in Engineering". Volume 2, Number 4, August 2012

[xv] Figueroa, Tanya, Hurtado, Sylvia, and Wilkins, Ashlee. "Black STEM Students and the Opportunity Structure". University of California, Los Angeles. Association for Institutional Research (AIR). Denver, Colorado, May, 2015.

[xvi] Cook, Lindsey. "Beyond the Headline: US Census Study on STEM Graduates". US News & World Report News. © July 16, 2014. http://www.usnews.com/news/blogs/data-mine/2014/07/16/beyond-the-headline-us-census-study-on-stem-graduates.

[xvii] The Big Bang Theory is a TV show about a group of friends who are mostly young scientists. The show premiered in 2009 on the Columbia Broadcasting System (CBS) network. It is the #1 comedy show on network television.

[xviii] Ortez, Fiona, "Chicago school closure battle intensifies with hunger strike". Reuters, August 28, 2015.

[xix] Layton, Lyndsey. "Chris Christie's bold plan to remake public schools is running into trouble". The Washington Post, March 3, 2015.

[xx] Raguso, Emille, "Berkeley School Board Primer: Berkeley Technology Academy review, council asked to move to Bonar, more." August 26, 2015.

[xxi] "The Burke Dilemma, What are we going to do about Burke High School?" The Post and Carrier, August 28, 2015.

[xxii] United Methodist Communications, Office of Public Information, "United Methodist HBCUs recruit minorities to STEM", October 1, 2013.

[xxiii] Michigan State University. "Parents still major influence on child's decision to pursue STEM careers". Science Daily, February 21, 2010.

[xxiv] Jascik, Scott." Missing minority Ph.Ds". Inside Higher Ed., November 3, 2014.

[xxv] Dr. Huxtable is a character from The Cosby Show which aired on 1984-1992 on the American Broadcasting Company (ABC). Recent controversy surrounding the show is not endorsed by this book.

[xxvi] The Big Bang Theory is a Central Broadcasting System (CBS) television show. Synopsis of the comedy television series can be found at URL: http://the-big-bang-theory.com/about/.

[xxvii] Whitehouse Google+ Hangouts Series. "We the Geeks". https://www.whitehouse.gov/blog/2015/02/23/telling-untold-stories-african-americans-stem.

[xxviii] US Department of Education. "Digest of Education Statistics". National Center for Education Statistics at the Institute of Education Sciences, 2013.

[xxix] National Center for Education Statistics. Institute of Educations Sciences. wwwhttp://nces.ed.gov/fastfacts/display.asp?id=667.

[xxx] HBCU-Levers Blog. http://hbcu-levers.blogspot.com/p/using-data-from-ipeds-data-center-this.html.

[xxxi] Mendoza, Martha, "Google Is Embedding Engineers At HBCUs To Fix Tech's Diversity Problem". Associate Press, May 3, 2015.

[xxxii]. Hefling, Kimberly and Elliott, Philip, "APNewsBreak: Koch Gift, UNCF to receive $25 million". Associated Press Newswire, June 6, 2014.

[xxxiii] The largest college endowment for HBCUs and MSIs is from Bill and Camille Cosby ($40 million) made in the spring of 2014 to Spelman. By comparison, John Paul, a hedge fund owner, donated $400 million to Harvard University (a predominantly white institution) in June 2015. This level of difference is common between black and white donors.

[xxxiv] Excerpt from US Department of Education Secretary Arne Duncan speech at the National HBCU Week Conference, September 26, 2013.

[xxxv] Anderson, Nick, "Feds announce new experiment: Pell grants for prisoners". The Washington Post, July 31, 2015.

[xxxvi] National Association for the Advancement of Colored People, "Know Your Worth, If We Don't Know We Can't Grow Our Community." http://www.naacp.org/entry/know-your-worth-if-we-dont-know-we-cant-grow-our-community.

[xxxvii] African American Registry. "Modjeska Simkins, Reformer and Civil Rights Leader"., 2000-2013.

[xxxviii] The State Newspaper. "Historical marker unveiled at former Victory Savings"., February 24, 2014.

[xxxix] "True Reformers Bank, The (1888 – 1910)". www.BlackPast.org.

[xl] Ready, Douglas A. and Truelove, Emily, "The Power of Collective Ambition". Harvard Business Review, December, 2011, pages. 1-10.

[xli] "Sapphire" is the name for describing black women believed to be sexually active and emasculating of their black male counterparts. It is a racist insult.

[xlii] The Manhattan Project was the atomic bomb research and development project during World War II.

[xliii] Mai-Cutler, Kim, "East of Palo Alto's Eden: Race and the Formation of Silicon Valley". TechCrunch, January 10, 2015.

[xliv] Ibid.

[xlv] Gannes, Liz, "What's Driving The Next Detroit? Part I of the Detroit Special Series". <Re/code> E-magazine, February 9, 2015.

[xlvi] Lyle, Caroline "10 EdTech Players Establishing D.C. As A Leader in Education". DCInno, October 2, 2014.

[xlvii] Weinberg, Cory, "College Fund Tinkers With Its Slogan to Stress Investing in Students". The New York Times, Bottom Line Section, June 16, 2013.

[xlviii] Luhby, Tami, "Worsening Wealth Inequality by Race". CNNMoney, June 21, 2012.

[xlix] Liquid wealth is defined as cash readily available on hand or easily accessible in a checking or savings account of a financial banking institution.

[l] "Beyond Broke: Why Closing the Racial Wealth Gap Is A Priority for National Economic Security". Center for Global Policy Solutions in collaboration with the Carolina Population Center at the University of North Carolina, the Research Network for Racial and Ethnic Inequality at Duke University, and the Milano Graduate School of International Affairs, Management and Urban Policy at the New School, and the Ford Foundation, 2014.

[li] United States Department of Agriculture, Center for Nutrition Policy and Promotion, "Official USDA Food Plans: Cost of Food at Home at Four Levels, US Average". January 2014, Alexandria, VA, February 2014.

[lii] Prudential Insurance Inc., "African Americans Making Financial Progress but Still Facing Financial Challenges", 2013 Prudential Research Study.

[liii] Hiltonsmith, Robert, "At What Cost? How Student Debt Reduces Lifetime Wealth". Demos.org, New York City, 2013.

[liv] Malcolm, Lindsey E. and Dowd, Alicia C. "The Impact of Undergraduate Debt on the Graduate School Enrollment of STEM Baccalaureates". The Review of Higher Education. Vol.35, Number 2. Pages 265-305, Winter 2012

[lv] Oliver, Melvin L. and Shapiro, "Black Wealth/White Wealth, A New Perspective on Racial Inequality". Thomas M. Routledge Publishing, 1995.

[lvi] Marketing Charts, "African-Americans and Hispanics Combine For One-Fifth of Estimated National Discretionary Spending", April 11, 2014.

[lvii] The Cable Advertising Bureau, "2014: The Year of the Black Consumer". ReachingBlackConsumers.com, 2014.

[lviii] Ellman, Stuart, RRE Ventures, "How Much Does A Startup Need?". Business Insider Magazine, Sept. 26, 2013.

[lix] National Science Board, National Science Foundation, "Science and Technology Indicators 2004, Venture Capital and High-Technology Enterprise Report", 2004.

[lx] Frey, William H., "Census 2000 Shows Large Black Return to the South, Reinforcing the Region's 'White-Black' Demographic Profile". Population Studies Center at the Institute for Social Research, University of Michigan and Milken Institute. Report No. 01-473, May 2001.

[lxi] Stoll, Michael A., "Great Recession Spurs a Shift to Local Moves. Department of Public Policy and Luskin School of Public Affairs", University of California-Los Angeles, February 2013.

[lxii] Kerr, William R., Lerner, Josh, and Schoar, Antoinette, "The Consequences of Entrepreneurial Finance: A Regression Discontinuity Analysis". Harvard University, 2010.

[lxiii] The authors of Black STEM USA are suggesting this name in recognition that the southeastern states tend to be more rural and is also a historical reference to the slave work in the fields of the south.

[lxiv] American Life Histories, Manuscripts from the Federal Writers' Project, 1936-1940, Progressive Era to New Era, 1900-1929, Prohibition: A Case Study of Progressive Reform, Harlem Rent Parties, Library of Congress, Manuscript Division, WPA Federal Writers' Project Collection.

[lxv] For Earlyshares and AngelList, investors must be "qualified" or accredited. For Crowdfunder, a minimum investment requires $1,000.00 to invest into a particular project promoted on the site.

[lxvi] Massolution®. "2013CF-The Crowdfunding Report", 2013

[lxvii] Barnett, Chance. "Top 10 Crowdfunding Sites for Fundraising". © Forbes Magazine, May 8, 2013.

[lxviii] Rewards-based funding is when investors receive "rewards" or small tokens of appreciation as "rewards" from the startup with which they invest. The rewards provided replace actual ownership in the company.

[lxix] 2014 data from Kickstarter.com.

[lxx] Kickstarter Creator Handbook, 2014.

[lxxi] Littlefield, Nick, "Kickstats: 4 Things You Need to Know about the Demographics of Crowdfunding". www.crowdlifted.com , November 20, 2013.

[lxxii] 2014 Data from www.quantcast.com, May 10, 2014.

[lxxiii] Goldstein, Jessica. "LeVar Burton: Criticism of Reading Rainbow Is 'Bullsh*t'" ThinkProgress, June 4, 2014.

[lxxiv] Covert, Bryce. "Americans Would Rather Do Business With White People Than Black People". ThinkProgress e-Magazine. © May 30, 2014. The article includes discussion and data showing that blacks also prefer doing business with whites.

[lxxv] PhD. Mollick, Ethan R., "Swept away by the Crowd? Crowdfunding, Venture Capital, and the Selection of Entrepreneurs". University of Pennsylvania Wharton School, March 25, 2013.

[lxxvi] Baker, C. Daniel, "Did a Kickstarter Project Bankrupt on Entrepreneur? What happens when you don't deliver your KickstarterProject?", January 18, 2013.

[lxxvii] "Kickstarter Creator Handbook", June 2014.

[lxxviii] Dr. Kevin Clark, PhD. was recently named a "Champion of Change" and received honors at the US Whitehouse.

[lxxix] Bishop, Jerry E., "The Media and Communicating Science to the Public". The Wall Street Journal. New York, New York, 1997.

[lxxx] Bosker, Bianca, "Why are African Americans More Likely to join Twitter?" The Huffington Post, Tech Section, June 16, 2014.

[lxxxi] *100Kin10* refers to Whitehouse-led initiative for an increase of 100,000 STEM teachers in 10 years. The end period of the initiative is CY2021.

[lxxxii] Wyss, Vanessa L., Huelskamp, Diane, and Seibert, Cathy J., "Increasing middle school interest in STEM careers with videos of scientists". International Journal of Environmental & Science Education. Pages 501-522.Vol. 7, No. 4., October 2012.

Made in the USA
Middletown, DE
11 May 2021